42

Middlesbrough
&
Teesside Memories

The publishers would like to thank the following companies for their support in the production of this book

Main Sponsor

Corus Teesside Cast Products

Atha & Co. Solicitors

David Fox Transport

Emanuel Spence Ltd

Greco Brothers

Hertel Uk Ltd

Huntsman Pigment Division

Lithgow Sons & Partners

Middlesbrough College

Parson & Crosland Ltd

P D Ports

R C Ayers Building & Roofing

Relph Funeral Services

Ridsdale & Co Ltd And Bureau of Analysed Samples Ltd

St. Mary's College

Suggitts Ice Cream Ltd

The Mall, Middlesbrough

University of Teesside

First published in Great Britain by True North Books Limited
England HX3 6AE
01422 344344

ISBN 1 903204 97 6

Text, design and origination by True North Books
Printed and bound by The Charlesworth Group

Middlesbrough & Teesside Memories

CONTENTS

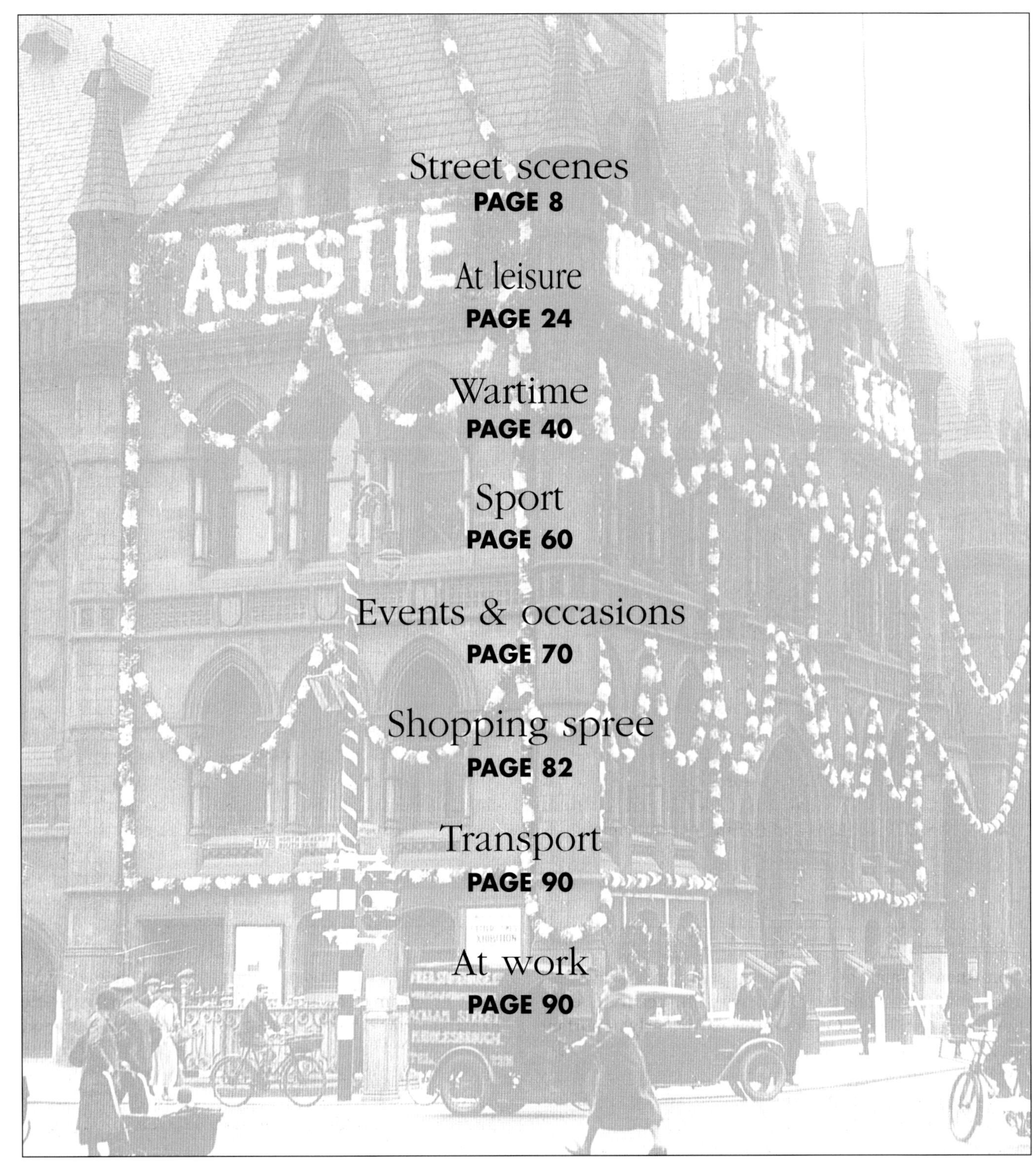

INTRODUCTION

You are about to enter a wonderland of nostalgia as you turn page after page of stunning photographs, all carefully captioned with descriptive text that is informative, thought provoking and, at times, quite pointed. We make no apology for wallowing in the past, because that is the nature of this book and its many companions across the country that are brought to you by True North publications. 'Memories of Middlesbrough and Teesside' will have the reader sharing in the days when trams rolled down our high streets, large family-run department stores had their own individual styles, children knew their times tables and we holidayed at Redcar, Seaton Carew and Saltburn. Taking a stroll down memory lane is something that we all enjoy doing. Some of us have a longer path to travel than others, but we are all fascinated by the recent history of times that are only just out of reach. These are particularly important when linked with the past of our own beloved town and its environs. Sadly, when we were young we often took only passing notice of the recollections that an older generation had to share with us, leaving but a sketchy awareness of those former days. Even our own firsthand knowledge can become clouded as we try to recall events, people and places as they used to be. Fortunately, for those who love to indulge themselves in nostalgia, this book will help jog the memory and bring back to life those days that helped shape our society in the last century.

The recorded history of Teesside really began with the invading Romans who built their first fort in the region in the Piercebridge area, just west of Darlington around 70AD. They stayed and held sway over the area for nearly three and a half centuries, before returning home to defend their own city that was under threat of major attacks. Stockton-on-Tees and Darlington were among the main settlements in the area in earlier times, both being Saxon settlements. The manor of Stockton was created in around 1138 and was purchased by Bishop Pudsey of Durham in 1189. It was granted a market charter in 1310, confirming its important status, but it was still not much more than a small port for many centuries. Darlington, also a medieval market town, with its beautiful early English St Cuthbert's Church, grew particularly important in the 19th century, thanks to the burgeoning railway industry that saw the development of large locomotive works here. Of course, the Stockton to Darlington Railway hosted the world's first passenger train in 1825.

Middlesbrough, in contrast, hardly existed at the start of

the 1800s, being a tiny hamlet of about 25 inhabitants, living in four farmhouses, though the place name 'Mydilsburgh' had been used over a thousand years earlier. However, its rapid growth was sparked by the actions of a group of Quaker businessmen, led by Joseph Pease, who saw the opportunity of building a large port at the mouth of the Tees to export coal from the Durham coalfields, using the new rail system to get the coal from the mines to the dockside. Discovery of ironstone in the Eston Hills helped found another major industry and Middlesbrough grew out of all recognition from the four initial streets, leading into the Market Square, that were initially laid out in c1829. The prophetic words attributed to Pease, 'Yarm was, Stockton is, Middlesbrough will be', became very true.

You are now nearly ready to turn the first page and bring back memories of the area as it was before the supermarket ruled our shopping patterns and satellite television consigned us all to the couch for our entertainment. Now use your imagination and the images provided to turn your attention to elegant buildings, jaunty shop awnings and people who talked of shillings and pence, quarts and gills, furlongs and yards. Put a stack of Film Fun comics and Famous Five books by your side to heighten the experience. Turn on the wireless for 'Workers' Playtime' or place on the gramophone a 78 record of Nat 'King' Cole singing 'Unforgettable'. With a glass of cream soda in one hand, a Kensitas cigarette dangling from the fingers of the other and a bag of misshapes from the sweetie shop on your knee, it is time to go begin. Become an Ovaltiney once more or pin on that Robertson's golly badge. Get in the mood and let 'Memories of Middlesbrough and Teesside' bring it all flooding back.

Captain James Cook - Middlesbrough's Greatest Son

Britain is an island nation with a naval history rivalled by very few. It has thrown up a number of figures who have claimed their places in the sea going hall of fame. Francis Drake's exploits on the Pelican or Golden Hind that saw him circumnavigate the world and his famed game of bowls before helping to scatter the Spanish Armada are real Boys' Own stuff. Horatio Nelson's leadership and bravery during the Napoleonic Wars that climaxed at Trafalgar is honoured by his own day on 21st October each year. In latter times, the single handed achievements of yachtsmen Francis Chichester and Alec Rose have captured the public imagination. Our own east coast has seen its fair share of nautical action, whether it be Vikings arriving on their missions of pillage and plunder, German U-boats shelling our ports or Grace Darling rowing out to the crew of the Forfarshire. However, this part of our country was also the birthplace of the sailor who can stand shoulder to shoulder with Drake and Nelson to claim the title of Britain's most influential sea captain. Cook is considered to have been Middlesbrough's greatest son and his name is associated with, streets, buildings and shopping centres. All over North Yorkshire and Cleveland, from Middlesbrough to Great Ayton, Redcar to Marske and Staithes to Whitby, there are places with Cook conections to explore.

James Cook was born at Marton on 27th October 1728, one of the five children of a Scottish farm labourer. The family moved to Great Ayton when Cook was seven and he attended the local school, where he learned the basics of mathematics, before leaving the village in 1745 to take up an apprenticeship as a haberdasher in Staithes. However, he was unsuited to this trade and went to Whitby and joined the merchant navy under the patronage of Captain John Walker. He continued to study algebra, trigonometry, navigation, geometry and astronomy. These subjects would stand him in good stead when the time came to take up command of his own ship. Cook worked on trading ships, particularly in the Baltic, and progressed in his profession to the rank of Mate on a collier by 1752. Three years later he decided to join the Royal Navy, though had to start again on the career ladder as an able seaman. He soon leapfrogged others, drawing upon his naval experience and educational background, to be given command of HMS Solebay and saw action in the Seven Years' War. His surveying skills were called upon when he was asked to map Newfoundland during his service there in the 1760s.

By now, Cook was filled with enthusiasm for exploring the wider world. He vowed to 'go farther than any man has been before me, but as far as I think it is possible for a man to go.' It was time to set off on the first of three great voyages that would make his name and earn him a place in the history books. In 1766, the Royal Society commissioned him to journey to the Pacific and track the movement of Venus across the Sun. His own interests in exploration led him to broaden his brief and he sailed Endeavour to New Zealand and proceeded to map the whole coastline before heading west to Australia. He made landfall on 29th April 1770 at the spot he christened Botany Bay, in honour of Joseph Banks and his colleagues who retrieved unique specimens of flora from the new continent. It was over a year later that the expedition finally made it back to Britain. He published his journals and took the first step towards celebrity status.

James Cook began his second voyage in command of Resolution in 1772, determined to explore further southern reaches of the globe. He crossed the Antarctic Circle in an attempt to discover Terra Australis, a mythical continent believed to lie below the only partially explored Australia itself. Realising that this was a fruitless exercise, Cook headed for warmer climes and made landfall at the Friendly Islands, Easter Island, Norfolk Island, New Caledonia and Vanuatu. Use of a much improved chronometer helped him accurately map the ocean and the lands he encountered. Some of these charts were still in use in the 20th century. On his return, he was made a Fellow of the Royal Society. But the call of the sea was too much. Cook was lured out of semi retirement to command Resolution once more in an attempt to discover the Northwest Passage. He explored the west coast of North America, but was frustrated in his attempts to get through the Bering Strait. Cook turned south and headed for Hawaii, where he was treated by the natives as some form of god. After effecting repairs to his ship, he set sail, but had to return shortly afterwards on 14th February 1779 when the foremast broke. Unhappily, local villagers were accused of theft from the ship and an argument ensued that got out of hand. In the skirmish, Cook was killed by a blow to the head. His memorial in Stewart Park was erected by HWF Bolckow of Marton Hall in 1858 to mark the site of the cottage where James Cook was born. The bicentenary celebrations, held on the park lawns on 8th September 1928, showing Bolckow's granite urn in the background, attracted huge numbers paying homage to the man who left a valuable legacy to the worlds of geography, botany and navigation. Nathaniel Dance's portrait of the great man hangs in the National Maritime Museum, Greenwich. In 1933 the cottage where the Cooks lived in Great Ayton was taken down and sent in barrels and cases to be reconstructed in Melbourne, Australia, where it is a popular tourist attraction.

STREET SCENES

How exciting it must have been to live in Victorian times. All right, we know all about the high rate of infant mortality, long and arduous working hours and conditions, poor sanitation and the class struggle, but what about technological advances? When the young queen took to her throne in 1837, Britain was still in the stages of metamorphosis from an agricultural society to an industrial one. The railway, still in its infancy, would expand dramatically, whisking people away from the places where their families had lived for generations to pastures, or more accurately townships, new. Then there were the mighty ocean going iron ships built by such visionaries as Brunel and steam replacing sail as the main power source. Gas lighting was introduced to their streets and homes and they had even heard that some German chappies called Daimler and Benz had produced some form of horseless carriages that they thought might make a useful addition to private transport. They used the telephone and telegraph, plus this new fangled electricity that some of them had come across. Here was an example of it in use on Newport Road in 1896 as the first trams clanked their way on tracks taking them past enthusiastic crowds lining the street. So much change and Britain was at the forefront of much of it. The Victorian age was truly golden.

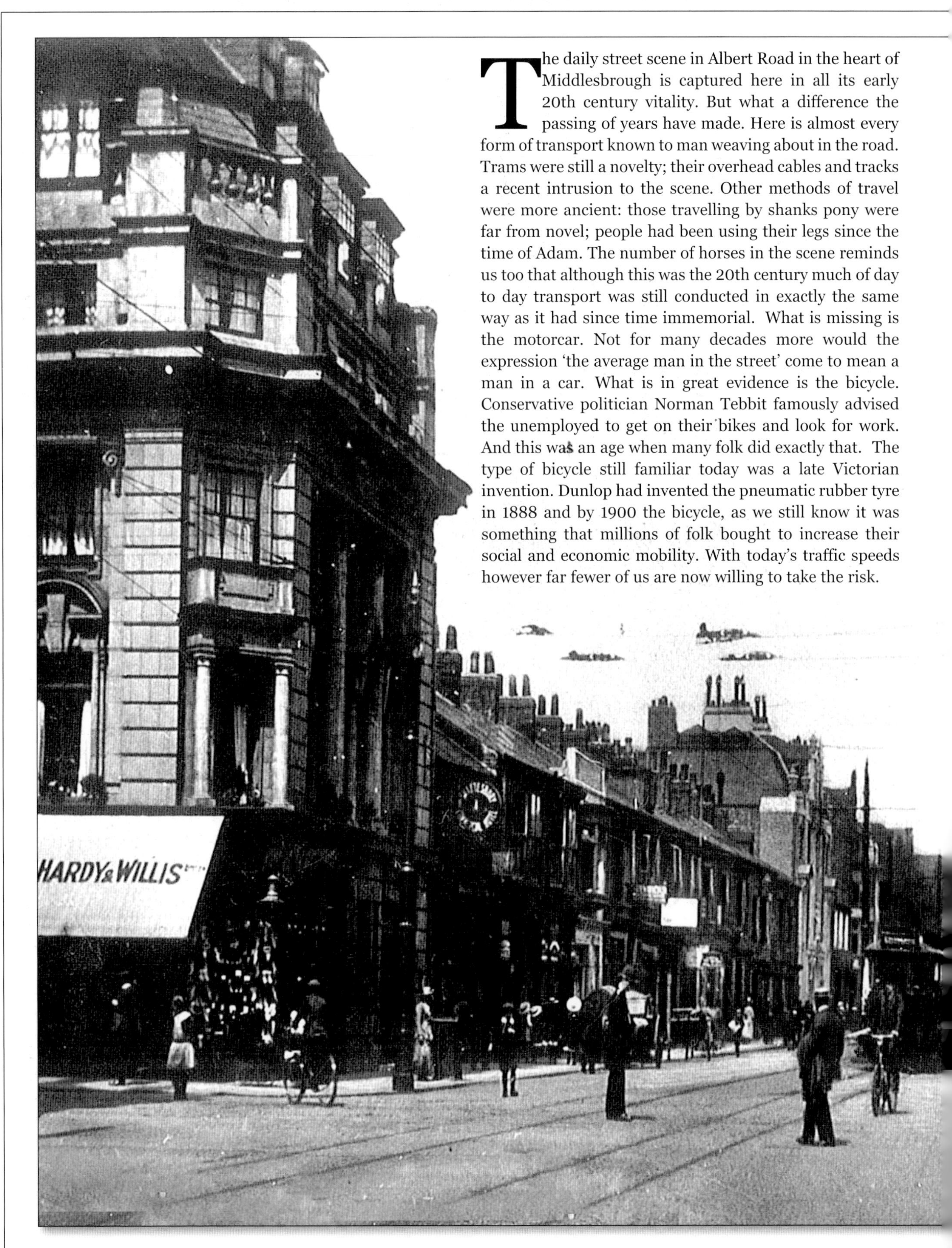

The daily street scene in Albert Road in the heart of Middlesbrough is captured here in all its early 20th century vitality. But what a difference the passing of years have made. Here is almost every form of transport known to man weaving about in the road. Trams were still a novelty; their overhead cables and tracks a recent intrusion to the scene. Other methods of travel were more ancient: those travelling by shanks pony were far from novel; people had been using their legs since the time of Adam. The number of horses in the scene reminds us too that although this was the 20th century much of day to day transport was still conducted in exactly the same way as it had since time immemorial. What is missing is the motorcar. Not for many decades more would the expression 'the average man in the street' come to mean a man in a car. What is in great evidence is the bicycle. Conservative politician Norman Tebbit famously advised the unemployed to get on their bikes and look for work. And this was an age when many folk did exactly that. The type of bicycle still familiar today was a late Victorian invention. Dunlop had invented the pneumatic rubber tyre in 1888 and by 1900 the bicycle, as we still know it was something that millions of folk bought to increase their social and economic mobility. With today's traffic speeds however far fewer of us are now willing to take the risk.

Above: Church Street/Market Place was a good spot to congregate and chat about the world, as these men demonstrated in 1920. For quite a few of them, talking was about all they had to do. They came home from the war expecting that the government would be grateful for the service they had given. Perhaps it was, but concrete evidence was hard to come by. There was David Lloyd George's hollow promise of 'homes fit for heroes', but reality proved to be something else. Work was not plentiful and got worse as the decade developed. Guisborough, along with many other market towns, changed in nature during the industrial revolution as its proximity to the ironstone deposits that were unearthed saw men leaving the land and heading for the mines and associated industries. One of the country's leading ironfounders, Joseph Pease, made Guisborough his country seat at Hutton Hall, by Hutton Lowcross. The town market, though, continued to flourish and was a focal point for the surrounding area. Cattle and other livestock were sold here, though nowadays it is fruit, vegetables, flowers and clothing that dominate the stalls. The town does not have a thoroughfare named High Street, but Westgate fulfils this function. Some of the smaller streets leading off take shoppers to specialist establishments that include Chaloner Street and Chaloner Mews, with its distinctive flower beds and cobbles.

Above: Victoria Bridge, Stockton stands as a tribute to the engineering skills of our 19th century forefathers. It opened on 20th June 1887, marking Queen Victoria's golden jubilee year, and replaced a stone one that dated from 1769. Car No 31 was on its maiden journey across the bridge on the Norton to Middlesbrough route on 16th July 1898, the day on which the Imperial Tramways Company launched its electrified service. The bridge still shows some of the shrapnel damage caused during an air raid in late August 1940. Holes can still be seen at the Thornaby end of the structure nearly half a century later. The night attack resulted in the first civilian death from enemy action in the area. Bombs aimed at the bridge or Thornaby Station damaged a nearby factory and left craters in Mandale Road and Thornaby Road. By then, trams had ceased to run anywhere in the Middlesbrough and Stockton district, having been phased out before the war. The local authorities of Middlesbrough, Stockton-on-Tees and Thornaby had bought out Imperial Tramways in 1921. The latter two combined as an operator while Middlesbrough went its own way, changing its Department name from Tramways to Transport in 1933. Larger motor buses had been purchased and gradually took over the role of the ageing trams as they were much more reliable and more cost effective.

Below: Seen in 1928, the Sussex Street subway provided a connection between the old part of the town and more recent developments on the other side of the railway. The attractive ironwork on the bridge is an example of the care the Victorians took in making their structures appealing as well as practical. No plain girders for them. The cyclist who had just passed underneath used a popular form of personal transport to get around. Cars were for the middle classes and the cost of motoring far out of reach of the hoi polloi. The sign above the roadworks, cautioning drivers to take care, was hardly necessary. It merely stated the obvious, but how our highways' managers love to erect such things. The road user of 80 years ago was not bombarded in the same way. Unfortunately, he had more to think about. These were difficult times as the depression years kicked in with a vengeance. The General Strike of 1926 showed just how unhappy the ordinary man was with his lot and soon the world would reel from the financial disaster of the crash on Wall Street in 1929.

Right: The Oxford Music Hall can be seen in the background of this old photograph. The clothes worn by these children and their parents certainly take us back at least a century to when Tyne Street was one of those side streets that connected Lower Faversham Street and Bridge Street East. No tumble driers back then, of course. Such machines were part of the fantasy world for families living in such conditions. Electricity had hardly reached the working classes, never mind the white goods that we all take for granted in our centrally heated homes that are adorned with every electrical and technological gadget you can think of. For poor old mum in those far off times, washing was aired on the line across the street. At least she did not have to worry about such things as motor cars coming past to pollute her dancing smalls, though the smoke and grime in the air from heavy industry was another matter. Life expectancy in cramped housing conditions, before the advent of penicillin, mass inoculation and modern antibiotics, was low. However, children played safely in front of their own front doors and, although they were poor, there was a sense of neighbourliness and community about such streets as this one. Although everyone knew everyone else's business, this had a plus side to it. Whenever someone needed a helping hand, there was always one on offer.

Left: Winterschladen's, the wine merchant, occupied a prime spot in the vaults under Middlesbrough Railway Station in c1920. As the name might suggest, the company's founder was of German origin. Joseph Winterschladen was born in Cologne in 1842 and came to England in 1865. He went into partnership with Uvo Pauls in 1868 as a wine importer, but went his own way in 1885 when he established the company that bore his name alone. He married a local girl in 1875 and they had eight children at Rhine Lodge, Marton Road. One of their descendants, Katy Winterschladen, born in 1984, is an up and coming actress and musician with television appearances that include 'Abigail's Party' and 'Casualty'. The railway station that we see here was badly damaged during the last war. In the summer of 1942, two bombs hit the centre of the roof, virtually destroying it in its entirety. A train bound for Newcastle, standing at the platform, was wrecked. However, it was not until 1954 that a major facelift was given to the station, at a cost of £70,000. Further alterations, particularly to the booking hall, occurred in 1978. The original building was a testament to the craft of our Victorian forefathers. Belonging to the North Eastern Railway Company, it was designed by William Peachey and opened for passenger transport in 1877, having cost £100,000.

Above: Trams ran along Mandale Road on the North Ormesby to Norton route from 1898 onwards. There was great exuberance surrounding the opening of the first electrified service on Teesside when excited onlookers, passengers and officials heralded the dawn of a new age, just right for the new century that would soon be upon them. It was thought that this would be the face of public transport in our towns for many decades to come, but the invention of the petrol engine was to bring a major rival to the tram in the form of the motor bus. After World War I, the increasing influence of the buses rang the death knell for our trams. The last of them made the run on the Linthorpe to Transporter route on 9th June 1934. Thornaby had seen many developments during its history and the tram was just one of them. Mentioned in the Domesday Book, it also has a noble connection with the Crusades. Robert de Thormodbi (an alternative spelling for the town) was wounded at Acre and swore an oath to build a shrine to the Blessed Virgin should he survive. He duly carried out his promise and a niche in honour of Mary, lit by five sanctuary lamps, was placed in the parish church of St Peter.

Victoria Square and the Municipal Buildings, overlooked by the graceful clock tower of the Town Hall are seen in this picture from the 1950s. The Central Library building is shown on the right of the picture, it was opened in May 1912, thanks to a £15,000 contribution by Andrew Carnegie the well-known philanthropist, and thanks also to the donation of a piece of land by Sir Hugh Bell. The Square itself had once been a cattle market, a skating rink and at another time served as the place where the circus was held. The Square as we know it now dates back to 1901 when it was opened by Colonel Sadler. The Town Hall dominates this picture. The Prince and Princess of Wales opened the grand £130,000 building in 1889.

Below: We do love a good disaster. Hence the rubber necking at motorway crashes, the ghoulish pilgrimages to houses where murders have been committed and, as in this case, where fire has broken out. It cannot have been too big an incident as there seems to be a lack of fire damage. Perhaps a cat had got stuck on the roof, but whatever the reason for the fire brigade to be in attendance at the property on Lord Street, the Redcar locals had come along to gawp rather than lend a hand. This was 1935 and, although motoring was beginning to take off in a big way as driving tests, cats' eyes and electric traffic lights were introduced, a significant proportion of those who had arrived at the scene had done so on their bikes. Cycling was both a popular sport as well as being a major form of transport over short distances. Several of the young girls in the photograph were dressed in a very modern fashion. Their shorts were just right for easy riding on their favoured form of locomotion. Older women, dressed in much fuller attire, even on such a warm day, wondered a little about the carefree and liberal attitudes of such pubescent young ladies. They thought that they might grow out of it and become more demure and retiring as they matured. No chance of that, of course, because a forthcoming war would need such strongminded girls to man the fort as their sweethearts went off to the front.

Above: This handsome view of the spectacular Middlesbrough Town Hall was taken one lunchtime c1960 when the traffic levels on Albert Road were much less than they became as the decade progressed. It was not just the vehicles and their numbers on the road that would alter during the next ten years. The fabric of British society underwent something of a revolution as the swinging 60s kicked in. It was a good time to be a baby boomer, one of those born in the immediate postwar years, because, as Bob Dylan would soon put it, 'The times they were a-changing'. We went into the decade as we started our teens and left it as young adults in our early 20s. That generation grew up in the austere period that still had rationing as it went off to primary school. As things got better during the Macmillan 'never had it so good' era of the late 50s, young people began to buck the trends and norms to which their parents had adhered. It showed itself at first in the type of music that teenagers enjoyed. Out went Dickie Valentine, Michael Holliday and other crooners. It was hip to be associated with Gene Vincent and Eddie Cochran instead and, as the 60s unfolded, even Elvis Presley became passé as the beat scene with home grown stars took over.

A crowded market scene recorded in the late 19505, looking north along the High Street. A rare view of Blacketts department store is given by the picture, seen here on the immediate right of the view. There were three large department stores at the time this picture was takenRobinsons Coliseum, Doggarts and Blacketts. Blacketts had formerly been D.Hill Carter & Co. LId before Blacketts took over, and later the business was acquired by Waring and Gill ow. Robinsons Coliseum eventually became Oebenhams. We shouldn't move on without mentioning the open-market traders, seen here with business in full swing. Market trading dates back around 700 years and has succeeded in attracting enough shoppers to the High Street to enable it to support the large stores already mentioned. The High Street began life as a residential area and became retail oriented later in its development. Of course, there was resistance to this from the residents of the street as the changeover took place, just as there was resistance from small retailers when the new developments came into town in the late 1960s and 1970s. Currently the debate is all about the effect that 'out of town' retail parks are having on the town centre's retail outlets. Perhaps, one day, we shall see our town centre's return to the residential function they performed over a century ago.

The year 1977 will be remembered by 'royal-watchers' for the Silver Jubilee of Her Majesty Queen Elizabeth II. The people of Stockton were honoured to learn that Her Majesty was to visit the town, as part of a tour of the north east, in July of that year. The tour began as the Royal Yacht Britannia sailed into Teesside, watched by thousands of well wishers. The Queen, accompanied by the Duke of Edinburgh, opened a new Tees Dock quay before moving on to visit the Prissick Base. After a visit to Durham the royal party went to Hartlepool where a new lifeboat was named. Throughout the tour the royal couple was accompanied by the Lord Lieutenant of Cleveland, Major Cecil Crossthwaite, along roads lined with thousands of flag-waving children adults and supporters of all ages. In Stockton people began to arrive in the town centre a full five hours before the Queen was due to arrive. The area was alive with activity; Council officials and staff clearing every last piece of litter and making sure that everything was in place for the big moment. Security staff and police officers making final checks to ensure the safety and security of the VIPs. There was a carnival atmosphere in the town, encouraged by the enthusiastic playing of the Billingham Solar Band and renditions of 'Viva Espania' to the delight of the onlookers. Overhead, cloudy skies threatened rain, but somehow this didn't prey on the minds of the swelling crowds too much. the High Street was filling up, most of the people lining the edge of the pavement around the Town Hall and along the street towards the Parish Church. People took advantage of every available square foot of elevated space to which they could gain access. Every window-sill, balconies, high walls and rooftops.

Above: The men anxiously checking the traffic as they cross Linthorpe Road need not do so any more, as this whole area is now pedestrianised. Shopping patterns have changed greatly in the years since this 1969 view was snapped as malls and arcades, such as the Hill Street Centre behind this row, have been added to the lines of individual shops we used to know. Whilst the premises have been retained, many of the names over the doors have changed. But not everything associated with the past has disappeared, for Marks and Spencer still trades from here, continuing to supply quality goods. The company has struggled, of late, weighed down by an image that it could not keep up with modern trends, especially in clothing. But, as the swinging 60s came to an end, it was very popular with those who wanted something other than the latest Carnaby Street fads. Mini skirts, hot pants and flowery patterns made their impact in boutiques then and in the early 1970s, but there was still a large market for practical and sensible clothing. Yet there was a swing towards more casual wear as men did not bother to come into town sporting ties, women dressed in trousers and children put on something other than their school uniforms.

Right: Opened to traffic on 28th February 1934 by the Duke of York, the Tees Newport Bridge spans the River Tees a short distance upriver from Middlesbrough Transporter Bridge, linking Middlesbrough with Stockton-on-Tees. Built by local company Dorman Long, who have also been responsible for such structures as the Tyne Bridge and Sydney Harbour Bridge, it was the first large vertical lift bridge in Britain. Constructed around twin 182ft (55m) lifting towers, the 270ft (82m) bridge span, weighing 2,700 tonnes, could be lifted by the use of two 325 H.P. electric motors at 52ft per minute to a maximum height of 120ft (37m). Originally 12 men would have been employed to man the bridge around the clock, usually requiring four to drive it at any one time. This was accomplished from the winding house situated midway along the bridge span. During the 1940s and early 1950s this would occur up to twice a day, however, as the number of ships needing to sail up to Stockton-on-Tees declined, so did the usage of the bridge. With the planned construction of the Tees Barrage heavy river traffic all but ceased and the decision was taken to seal the lifting span. The bridge

was raised and lowered for the last time in an informal ceremony on the 18th November 1990, this time with scores of people enjoying the ride. The span was subsequently bolted down. Newport Bridge still serves as a road bridge, carrying considerable traffic as a section of the A1032, despite the presence of the A19 Tees Flyover a short distance upriver.

Above: The Newport roundabout was featured in this picture from 1968 to illustrate a story about road improvements. At this time it had been estimated by the local authority that traffic delays cost Teesside around £380,000 per year - though it is not clear how the boffins had arrived at this figure! The new £55,000 works had been approved by the Highways Committee and were intended to speed the flow of vehicles through the notorious bottlenecks at Newport roundabout and the Ayresome Street - Acklam Road intersection.

AT LEISURE

Long before the package holiday to Benidorm was ever thought of, enjoying the sunshine close to home was the way Britons spent their leisure time. The railways opened up the country for us in Victorian times and motor transport added to the opportunities for travel. Even though that meant that we could move further afield in our search for relaxation, most viewed their journeys in tens of miles rather than in hundreds. Anyone living close to the coast need not go far. Anyone with access to the east coast resorts was well blessed. Along the shoreline on Wearside and Teesside there were marvellous beaches and in summer the sands at the Hartlepools, Seaton Carew, Marske and Saltburn were packed with holidaymakers and day trippers. Perhaps the premier place to be was Redcar. Here in 1925, looking east along the beach and Esplanade, we can see just how popular the resort was. In fact, there were so many that even the long expanse of sand could not cope and thousands simply promenaded along the front enjoying the sea air and the lovely views. It does seem quaint, when we take in the clothing that people wore on the beach, to see men in suits and women in coats. Sun worshipping was not the popular pastime that it became in the second half of the last century.

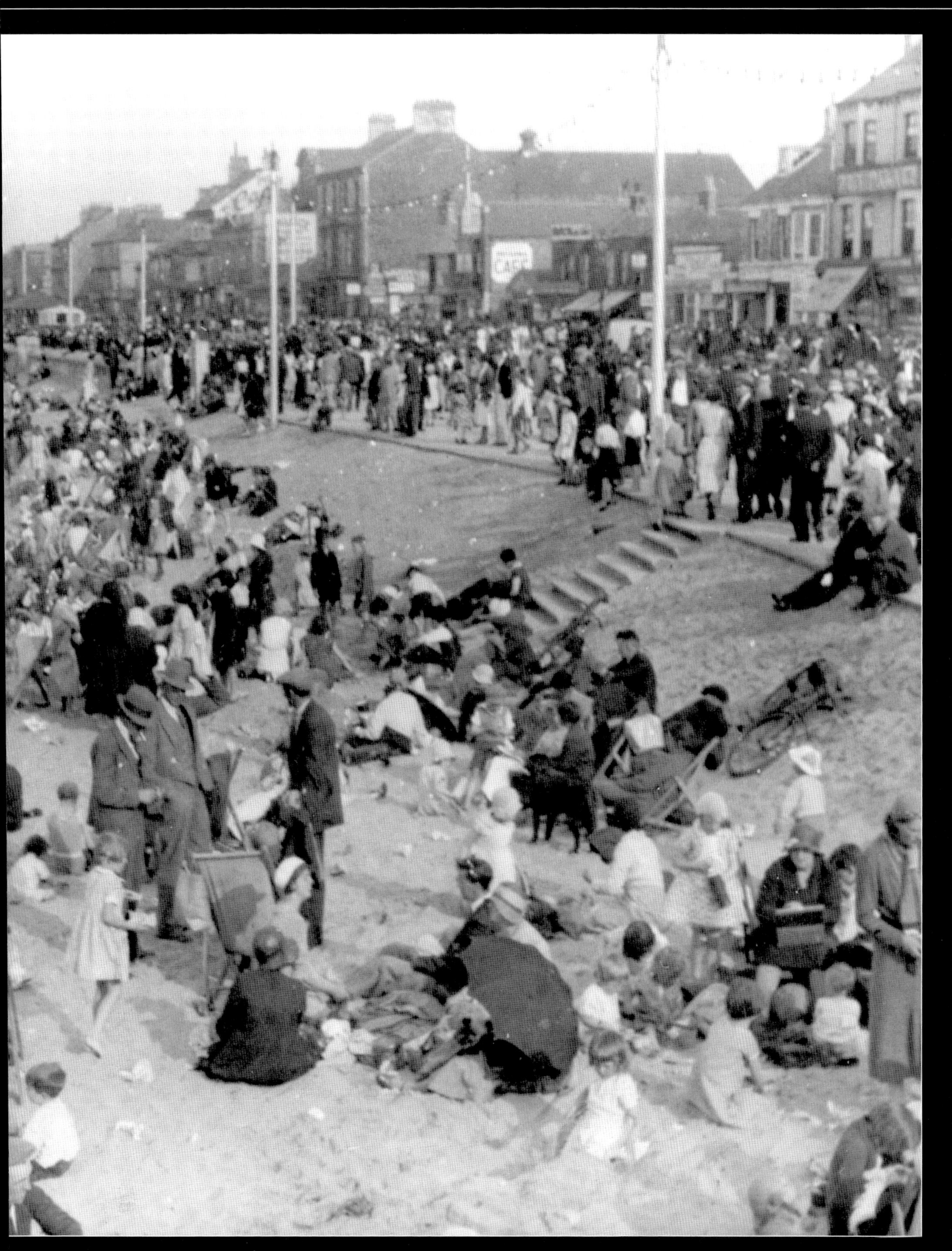

Above: In years to come, ladies would earn millions from their prowess at the game that Mark Twain described as 'a good walk spoiled'. Michelle Wie, Paula Creamer, Annika Sorenstam and the rest can live in luxury thanks to their prowess and good looks that have earned them assured futures. But, in 1930 there was no such money about for women's golf. There were some famous players, such as Glenna Collett and Diana Fishwick, but the professional game was still in its infancy and would not develop on any major scale until well after the war. That did not deter this pair on The Stray at Redcar. Presumably husband and wife, they enjoyed their round of miniature golf just as much as any Bobby Jones might have done. Perhaps the green could have done with a bit of a manicure, but the vagaries of the line only added to the amusement. Hubby, of course, was full of advice about backswing and follow through, but when she knocked in a 20 footer it was just beginner's luck. The coast at Redcar is a delightful place to stroll and enjoy the salty air. Our photographed couple, after putting their clubs away, could have wandered along the grassy area until they came to the Esplanade and enjoyed a quiet drop of refreshment before making their way home.

Left: Panning for gold in the waters of the North Sea at Redcar in c1935 was unlikely to hit pay dirt and turn the area into the Klondike, but you never know. These prospectors, earnestly examining their sieves and Sovereign cream wafer tin, were just as happy with the treasures that they discovered. Perhaps there was a little fish, a magically shaped tiny shell or even a sparkling fragment of a pebble to stir their imaginations and give them some excitement. How youngsters just love to root around in rock pools and at the water's edge. They can lose themselves in a world of their own make believe and oh how thrilled they are when they discover something out of the ordinary that they can pretend to be truly special. Rushing up to dad, last seen with his eyes firmly shut reclining in the striped deckchair in the distance, shouting 'Look what I have found' means that there is a special moment to be shared that every father cherishes. Secretly he might have wished for a few moments longer in reverie, but the sunny smiles on those bonny faces would melt the hardest of hearts. Naturally, he enthuses about the find and knows that somehow he is going to have to make sure that it gets safely back home or his little one will be heartbroken.

Above: These young ladies belonged to the generation that took women's lib much further than it had ever gone before and helped pioneer social changes greater than any that would come again. The bra burners of the 60s and 70s cannot compare with the achievements of these doughty folk. After the first world war, they threw off the shackles imposed upon them by their fathers. Their mothers had fought for the right to vote and had kept the wheels of industry turning while their husbands were away. Throughout the 1920s, these members of Redcar Amateur Swimming Club continued to chip away at the antiquated values of their fathers. They took jobs that gave them greater independence and finally secured equality in the polling booth. As 1930 dawned, they had cast off the sort of clothing that was literally straight laced and adopted freer styles that reflected their liberation in society. Women started to enjoy themselves in public and took up vigorous pastimes that had previously been classed as unladylike or too strenuous for such delicate constitutions. Our band of intrepid swimmers posed happily for this picture without any of the self conscious restraints that their mothers might have had. Their happy, smiling faces said it all. Why should men have all the fun? Fancy living by the seaside and not being able to enjoy the pleasures of a dip in the briny.

In recent years, Redcar has become a popular spot for diving devotees. However, such pieces of equipment as Scuba apparatus, flippers and wetsuits were not for this group of aquatic fans. Snorkelling was not on the agenda as they were more interested in the delights of the open air pool. Such swimming centres, also known elsewhere as lidos, were very popular in between the wars and continued to hold their position as premier league recreation well into the 1950s. Redcar's most famous spot, where any budding Johnny Weissmuller or Esther Williams could practise the art, was at Coatham Enclosure. It opened in 1930, the same year that the resort attracted some 36,000 visitors on Whit Monday. What a heaving mass of humanity that must have been. The swimming costumes worn at the pool, as one intrepid soul prepare to take the plunge off the equivalent of the high diving board, are almost unisex in the days before the term was coined. One piece top and bottom garb for men as well as women was the order of the day. How strange, that by the time the 1970s came along, the beaches, if not the pools, would see many women joining men by wearing one piece costumes once again. However, the difference was that both sexes had now discarded the top half of their apparel.

DAY NURSERY

Above: Red Rum used to train on Southport beach before his mighty exploits in the 1970s when he galloped to triple success in the Grand National. The sands are a good place to exercise horse, providing long stretches where the animals can stretch their legs and race freely. Modern trainers, such as Ferdy Murphy, continue to exercise their charges at Redcar and other resorts. The beach near here was used as a racetrack for many years. Until Squire Newcomen and the Earl of Zetland were able to establish the enclosed racetrack in the town, Coatham Sands was the place to go to enjoy the thrills of the sport of kings. Large numbers attended the racing in the early 19th century and the crowds were difficult to control. There were also some unruly scenes that caused the authorities nervous moments. Regulating open air events was difficult and quite often the meetings attracted unsavoury elements, with pickpockets having a field day. Unscrupulous bookies often disappeared without trace when a favourite romped home. An enclosed track meant that spectators could be given greater safety and their control was easier as well. The collection of entrance fees was made much simpler and helped increase the prize money that could be offered to attract a better standard of racehorse and jockey to compete at Redcar. The photograph dates from the early 1920s and shows a hunter being put through its paces as it was broken in.

Right: Perhaps it was not the best of days when this view across the beach was photographed. Nearly everyone is well wrapped up, but maybe the picture does not tell the entire story. This was the mid 1930s and we were not accustomed to stripping off quite as freely as we do today. Even when the sun shone brightly, it was something of a daring move if the missus pushed her skirt above her knees as she sat on the blanket she had brought with her. Her hubby's acknowledgement of the blazing orb in the sky was to roll up his shirtsleeves and produce a handkerchief with knotted corners that he plonked on his head. It must be admitted,

though, that at times as holidaymakers we endured the sort of weather that would have had our continental cousins scurrying to the bars and cafés along the seafront. The determined British took the stance that this was their week off from work and it had to be spent on the beach, come hell or high water, come rain or shine. The sands and the sea were there to be enjoyed, but accidents can happen. We did not have lifeguards and warning flags along our shores in those days, but there was always some measure of assistance available. The tent on the right was a small first aid shelter run by members of the St John Ambulance.

Right: Whatever is down there must be really fascinating. The little lad on the right had better take care or he will soon be joining Jaws or whoever is lurking in the depths of the rock pool. Mum told him to be careful, but boys will be boys and he would not worry too much if he overbalanced and went in. It is obviously something truly remarkable as he is not the only one who seems to be intent on determining the exact nature of the creature that lies below. Things have not changed much since 1935 and children still poke around on the seashore at Redcar today. What a simple pleasure it is. Mums and dads continue to join in as well, but not dressed in the same way as they were nearly three quarters of a century ago. It is incongruous to modern eyes to see a woman wearing her hat and firmly clutching her handbag while enjoying the delights of the seaside. Not only that, but she is also wandering across the rocky bits in her outdoor coat, stockings and everyday shoes. The men are also dressed just as they would be if out and about in town. Brogues on their feet, jacket and trousers on their bodies and, in some cases, still wearing their club ties, these chaps seem somewhat over attired for their day on the beach. But, that is how it was and that is what makes such nostalgic pictures interesting.

Above: 'It will all end in tears'. The usual admonition had been given, but the trio of children leaning forward as they looked down into the paddling pool on The Stray were not too worried if they fell in. The water was only a few inches in depth and they would come to little harm. Other youngsters ventured further out and encouraged toy sailboats to catch the breeze and drift across the surface. Parents sat idly by as their offspring indulged in harmless fun. This long stretch of grassy promenade between Marske and Redcar has always attracted people taking a stroll or enjoying a picnic in family groups. Young lovers could wander, arm in arm, as they gazed fondly at one another, oblivious to the world that was passing them by. Pacitto's ice cream parlour offered a delicious stopping off point on the way. One of the good things about the paddling pool in 1930 was that it offered free entertainment. The economic depression that affected the whole country and the northeast in particular meant that families had little money to spare, so something for nothing was very welcome. In recent times the area ahs been restocked with a new multi play centre, but The Stray is no longer the friendliest of places when it gets dark as vandals and louts seem to have made it their own.

Above right: All ready for the off, this party of well dressed racegoers was about to enjoy a day's racing at Redcar, 1920s style. Variously garbed in plus fours, three piece suits and hacking jackets, each man was officially hatted. It did not matter if it was bowler hats, homburgs or natty flat caps, it was not the done thing to be seen at the races without appropriate headgear, don't you know. These prosperous looking chaps did not mind a flutter as it was always seen to be part of the day's fun. To the lower classes, lurking well out of sight, a successful punt on the 3.30 might mean the difference between food on the table that evening or a rumbling stomach, yet again. This was the period when the years of depression began to take hold and there was a definite divide between the haves and have nots in this country. Not only was there a wide financial gap, there was a real class split. The 'toff', as anyone with money or airs and graces was known, was as far removed from the bottom strata of society as could be. Anyway, such people were just common, as far as he was concerned, and worthy of only scant regard.

Corporation houses were part of the town's growing stock of rented houses, built as part of the drive to replace the rows of badly maintained terraced property which had been the subject of a long running slum clearance programme. Attempts to upgrade the area's housing stock had been made throughout the 1950s and 60s. By 1964 a total of 2500 houses had been pulled down. Records from that year indicate that the Council's plan was to have all the slums cleared by 1968. This involved the removal of a further 2000 properties - a massive undertaking. There had been some considerable success in the provision of new council homes. By 1962 the council,was renting out a total of 8700 properties and over three-quarters of these were post-war in origin. Average rents in the mid-1960s were just £2 per week.

Below: This well-attended cricket match took place in the suburbs of Stockton in August 1964. These modern

This photograph dates from 1972, the films being shown at the time were Chisulll starring John Wayne, and when Dinosaurs Ruled the Earth starring someone else. At this time the world of entertainment was more interested in two new productions which had been launched onto the Arts scene. Lloyd Webber's musical Jesus Christ Superstar and Francis Ford Coppola's The Godfather were to have a much greater impact on the world of entertainment than the makers of When Dinosaurs Ruled the Earth could ever have imagined. At the time this scene was recorded this venue was operating under the ownership of the Essoldo Cinema, though the word Hippodrome was retained on the edge of the canopy in view of its original name when it opened in 1905. For some time the establishment traded as the Cannon before closing finally in the last quarter of 1993.

Ayresome Park has seen some crowds in its time. The terraces have been crammed, the crush bars threatening to buckle under the strain, as Wilf Mannion's skills lit up the play or Brian Clough arrogantly slotted in his five goals against Brighton in 1958. The roar of the crowd on those days was of a deeper tone than the decibel crunching screech from 20,000 children on 2 July 1930. They waved their flags and gave the adults with them severe headaches that took hours to recover from. There was good reason to be excited, the Prince of Wales was visiting. This was a time long before television, so the opportunity to see even images of royalty was limited. There were glimpses in cinema newsreels and photographs in newspapers, but the Royal Family was still sufficiently remote to be placed on an adoring pedestal. Little wonder that we went into a frenzy when there was the chance to see a royal in the flesh. In that between the wars era the monarchy was very popular, but the nation's affection and loyalty was to be sorely tested a few years later. When, in 1936, the Prince of Wales succeeded his father to the throne as Edward VIII his short reign was blighted by scandal. His involvement with the twice divorced American socialite, Wallis Simpson, split the country. Failing to win government and church support, he abdicated. Some of those who cheered him at Ayresome Park also jeered him off into exile.

Right: Now there's an intrepid young lady. She is risking having her toes nibbled by something or other in the rock pool. It appears as if she is none too certain about going any further and it could be that discretion will win the day. But, at least she tried and impressed the lads with her tomboy spirit. Different things were expected of the sexes when these children were growing up. Even though women were much more emancipated than they had ever been, a little girl was still expected to be more gentle and timid than her brothers. It was out of the ordinary for her to climb trees or get her knees dirty, while this was regarded as almost compulsory for any boy. He was also expected to be the one who was 'a little monkey' and he played up to it. A day at the seaside at Redcar in 1935 was not complete without young Johnnie creeping up behind his sister, shouting 'Watch out, there's a crab behind you' and then pinching her bottom. She immediately ran off to her mother, yelling those age old words that parents know all too well, 'Tell him, mum'. Of course, he was nowhere to be told anything, having made very sure that he was at the other end of the beach until the fuss died down.

Below: Now let us get one thing straight. Colonel Sanders has not come to town, so there will be no buckets of chicken and french fries today. However, if your mind was wandering across the big pond to Churchill Downs, the home of the Kentucky Derby, then you would be much nearer the mark. The horse and jockey portrayed outside the Regent Cinema were from the Redcar Riding School and were helping to advertise the main feature film of the week. The picture house opened in 1937 in the town centre, just over a year before 'Kentucky' was shown to packed houses. It starred a new name in Hollywood. Richard Greene was a young Devonian who had been signed by 20th Century Fox as a rival to MGM's Robert Taylor. He was an immediate success and his good looks brought female fans out in droves to swoon over him. At his peak, his fan mail outstripped that of Fox's other top star, Tyrone Power. 'Kentucky' was a modern Romeo and Juliet story, set in horse racing circles. The love interest was provided by Loretta Young, an actress who would win an Oscar in 1947. Walter Brennan completed the star line up. Greene's career was put on hold as he was on active service during the war and it never fully recovered. However, he became famous again in the late 1950s as Robin Hood in a television series that lasted for 143 episodes. The Regent closed in the 1960s.

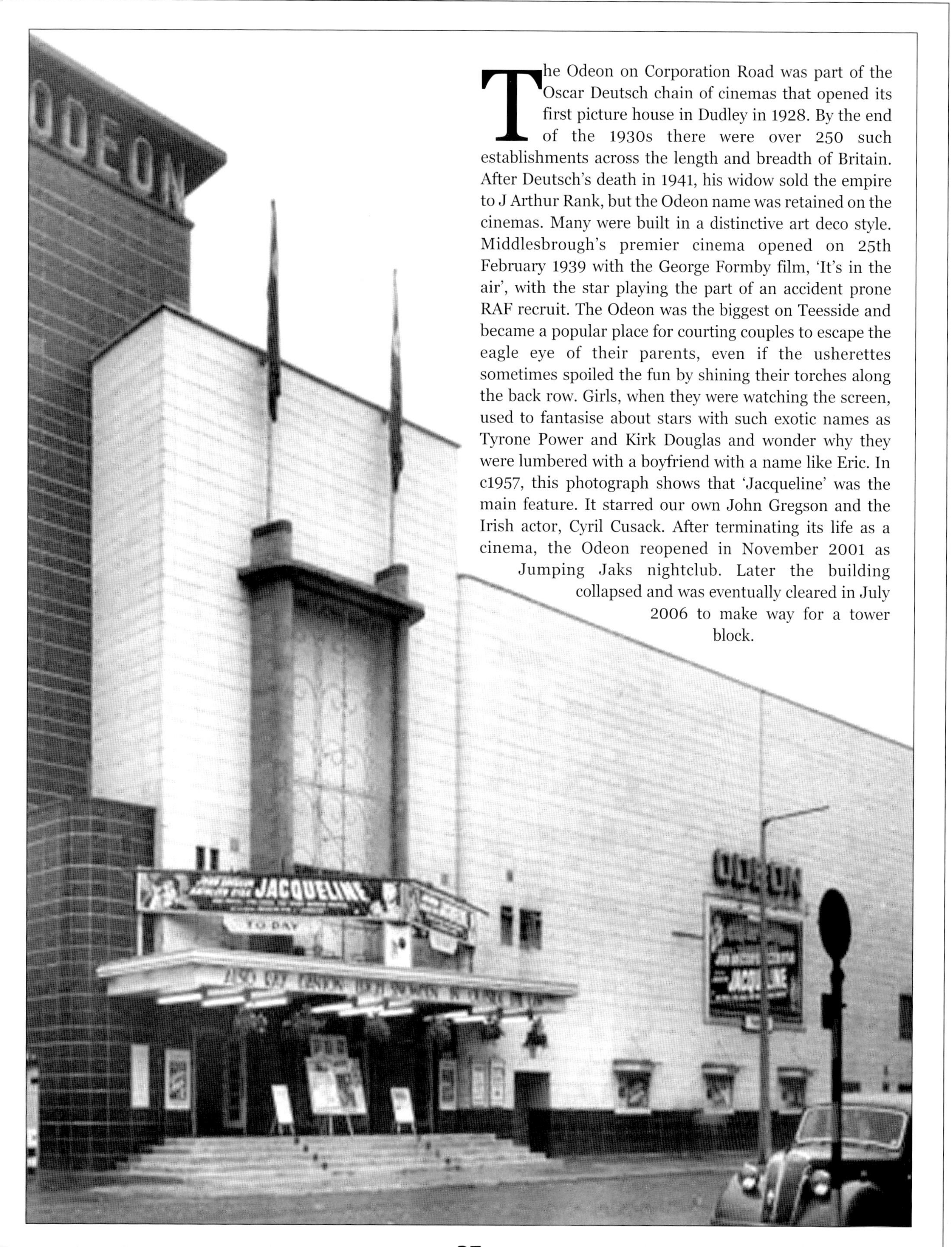

The Odeon on Corporation Road was part of the Oscar Deutsch chain of cinemas that opened its first picture house in Dudley in 1928. By the end of the 1930s there were over 250 such establishments across the length and breadth of Britain. After Deutsch's death in 1941, his widow sold the empire to J Arthur Rank, but the Odeon name was retained on the cinemas. Many were built in a distinctive art deco style. Middlesbrough's premier cinema opened on 25th February 1939 with the George Formby film, 'It's in the air', with the star playing the part of an accident prone RAF recruit. The Odeon was the biggest on Teesside and became a popular place for courting couples to escape the eagle eye of their parents, even if the usherettes sometimes spoiled the fun by shining their torches along the back row. Girls, when they were watching the screen, used to fantasise about stars with such exotic names as Tyrone Power and Kirk Douglas and wonder why they were lumbered with a boyfriend with a name like Eric. In c1957, this photograph shows that 'Jacqueline' was the main feature. It starred our own John Gregson and the Irish actor, Cyril Cusack. After terminating its life as a cinema, the Odeon reopened in November 2001 as Jumping Jaks nightclub. Later the building collapsed and was eventually cleared in July 2006 to make way for a tower block.

These photographs are a real trip down memory lane, though that should be the journey our grandparents took as most of these images come from the early 20th or late 19th centuries. That does not matter, as we all have recollections of how we spent our time in our youth or how our forefathers told us about what they did when they were young. The schoolroom is a good place to start. Where once there were slates and chalk, the next generation had the benefit of inkwells and dip pens that blotted alarmingly, earning the poor student a clip round the ear from the spinster in charge of the class. How lucky we were when reliable fountain and cartridge pens were introduced and we had the benefit of decent blotting paper. Boys and girls were given different goals to achieve. The lads were expected to become proficient in carpentry, as a worthwhile activity for the future man of the house. Of course, girls knew their place and they made sure that they knew how to use a sewing machine and bake a cake. Even in the 1970s, lads came home with pencil boxes that they had carved and their sisters wandered in from school with a square of binka cross stitching or half a dozen scones. Mums were jolly good at running things up on the Singer or clicking away with a pair of number 8 needles as dresses were made and cardies produced. No proper housewife wasted money on ready-made curtaining. She went to the market and bought a few yards of material, some lining and tape and got on with it herself. She might ask hubby to hold a ball of wool from time to time, or to lend a hand on the step ladder putting up the pelmet, but mum ran the house without too much assistance from any third parties. Mat making and rug weaving were other strings to their bows and patchwork quilts became standard issue as bedcovers.

Out in the playground or back home on the street, youngsters occupied themselves with games that needed little in the way of kit or equipment. Whatever they lacked, they were able to improvise. A game of football could be played with a bundle of rags tightly bound together, or an inflated pig's bladder, cadged from the butcher, could do the job. Games came in seasons. In the autumn, it was conkers. Cheats soaked theirs in vinegar and baked them in the oven before introducing them into the fray. There was many a tear shed when a prized 37-er was shattered by one that owed its power to a pickling in Sarson's and being heated up next to the Sunday joint. You needed the equivalent of a science degree to determine the precise moment to get them out before they exploded all over the basting tray and then it was dodge mum for the next half an hour, or else. Later in the year, we played marbles. Blood alleys, whiteys, big dobbers and stripeys all had their own special value. Circles were drawn in the dirt and earnest games of ringo contested. Swaps were allowed and the currency was sometimes keenly debated. Were three green glassies actually the same value as one Bill Edrich cigarette card? Discuss.

The school yard was a source of fun with plenty of chasing games. British Bulldog, tag and rally-o were great fun, as was the one that involved grabbing the girls' pigtails and tying them together. That usually got us the slipper, but only if someone squealed. Youngsters chalked squares on the flagstones and played hopscotch, they flicked jacks in the air as they bounced a little ball, tops were wildly whipped and two ball was played against the side of the infants' doorway. If you listened hard enough you could hear 'What time is it Mr Wolf?' being asked from one corner and 'Salt, mustard, vinegar, pepper' being chanted in another. At home we loved to make as much noise as we did on the playground. That is something that has not changed down the years. Very young children have always been fascinated by sound. The smaller their vocabulary, the more row they love to make. Give a kiddie a drum and he is as happy as Larry. Mum and dad may cringe, but the little one will have a whale of a time. Penny whistles and toy trumpets have a similar effect, both on the parents' nerves and on the scale of joy measured by the size of the smile on the little imp's face. We should be glad that schools introduce children to the recorder at an early age, rather than the euphonium. Our love of the sea as a leisure activity remains a constant, though we have paddled away on the sands in many different fashions. At one time, topless men were seen as being rather daring, racy souls. How would our Victorian forebears have responded to women peeling off their upper layers? No doubt Queen Victoria would have repeated her 'We are not amused' statement. Young women were very bold when they revealed their knees and arms to the world as their parents made sure that they disrobed and changed into bathing attire inside a machine that could be wheeled into the water. We can look back at the things people did in the past and smile at some absurdities, but we can bet that in 2100 our great grandchildren will be doing the same about us.

WARTIME

Residents on Wilson Street never forgot 3rd August 1942. That was the day that became forever etched in their memories as the Luftwaffe flew overhead and sent down its hail of death onto the town below. Houses on this street and in the vicinity were torn apart as explosions and fires laid them to waste. Looking towards the junction with Linthorpe Road, the level of devastation is plain to see. It

was during this attack that the railway station was destroyed when a Dornier dropped a stick of 17 bombs on its roof. By this time, locals had become used to the sound of the air raid siren since it had been sounded on numerous occasions since the early summer of 1940 when the first bombing raids were endured. However, familiarity did not breed contempt, just fear and anxiety. Residents made their way to cellars or Anderson shelters and waited for the all clear to be given. Then they made their way back to ground level, not knowing what they would find when they emerged from their hidey-holes. The saddest part of the assaults on our housing was not that buildings were destroyed, but that homes were lost. A house is a pile of bricks and mortar, but a home is a place full of fond memories and something a family has made together. They had no right to destroy that.

Above: Although 'Dad's Army', that brilliant BBC TV sitcom, was hugely amusing and so popular that it even spawned a movie, it did help to perpetuate the myth that the Home Guard was made up of buffoons and 'stupid boys'. When it was first screened in 1968, many former members who had served their country wrote irate letters to the 'Beeb'. It did, though, give people a chance to set the record straight with a younger generation that had grown up in the baby boomer years and did not know the background of the force. Initially known as the Local Defence Volunteers when formed in May 1940, Winston Churchill changed the name to Home Guard in August. It was formed when there was a real risk of invasion. Most men who could fight were already in the forces; those who were left were either too young, too old or in reserved occupations. Volunteers were expected to fight an invasion of crack German troops, but it has to be admitted that initially they were issued with a ridiculous collection of old shotguns and pieces of gas pipe with bayonets welded on the end. Some trained by marching with broomsticks over their shoulders, but gradually they were issued with proper weapons and underwent rigorous exercises. About 100 of Middlesbrough's battalions can be seen here marching past Albert Park, looking very professional in their manner.

Right: The watching crowd cheered the Airborne Troops of Northern Command who were on an exercise in late 1943. Some of these men had already marched 66 miles in just two days and were to be whisked away into battle almost immediately. They had been acting in conjunction with the Home Guard in protecting some of the vulnerable positions in the Middlesbrough and Stockton on Tees area. By then, the threat of a German invasion had passed and troops that had been retained to look after British installations could be released to join their comrades at the front. Remarkably, at the start of the war we had no parachute or paratrooper regiments. The Germans, though, used them to good effect and they fitted in well with the 'blitzkrieg' theory of swift attacks. Their regiments had gained experience on active service during the Spanish Civil War and they were used effectively in the assaults on Norway

and the Netherlands. The loss of a quarter of the force when attacking Crete in 1941 led to a loss of German confidence in paratroopers. Britain took an opposite path by introducing the first Airborne Division at the start of 1941 and deployed these troops in a number of situations until the heavy losses during the 1944 D-Day invasion and the failed Arnhem mission caused a rethink.

Right: Brambles Primary School is on Kedward Avenue, just off Cargo Fleet Lane, the A171 road to Ormesby. Now it is all SATs, Key Stages and league tables and little ones are labelled as being in foundation or reception classes. Still, when a youngster was once known as a 'mixed infant', we were given titles that were just as puzzling to us when taking our first steps up the educational ladder. Of course, the grey haired among us will tell you about the best years of our lives and how rosy things were when we were merrily playing British Bulldog and conkers in the playground before the health and safety mob moved in to ban such pursuits. We knew that eight sevens were fifty-six without the need of a calculator and that learning to read was a joy not a forced activity. But, stop for a moment and examine this photograph of these Bramble infants in 1939 and we will see that life was not quite the picnic we pretend it to have been in earlier times. War was only just over the horizon and the government, fearful of the use of gas or chemicals by attacking enemy forces, issued safety masks to all children. Schools and civil defence groups instructed them in their use as the nation readied itself for the sort of conflict when citizens as well as the armed forces would be in the front line and kiddies carried their masks in little cases to and from school each day.

Above: In September 1938, Britain entered the short period of prewar history that became known as the 'Munich crisis'. The previous month, Hitler began making speeches that made it clear that Germany was considering sending troops into Czechoslovakia. Six months earlier, Austria had been annexed and the western world was anxious to determine the extent of Nazi ambitions for the rest of Europe. The British prime minister, Neville Chamberlain, flew to Germany and met with the German Chancellor in an effort to defuse the situation. A further meeting was arranged for the end of the month and an agreement was drawn up whereby Hitler agreed to stay out of the rest of Czech territory, provided that the Sudetenland was returned to the Germans.

Chamberlain returned home, waving his now infamous piece of paper that contained a copy of the agreement. A week later, tanks rolled across the border, but did not stop there and within a few months they were in Prague. At the time of the Munich crisis, there were already plans in place known as the Air Raid Precautions (ARP), though response to the measure introduced in 1935 had been sketchy. Middlesbrough Town Hall had a thermometer that showed the number of volunteers who had joined. It was not an inspirational reading at the time of Chamberlain's appeasement exercise and ARP membership only got going with any great effect a year later.

Below: Redcar in wartime, as this picture from the early 1940s might be captioned, shows the clock tower and air raid shelters. The Grade II listed building, one of the town's focal points, underwent a £260,000 facelift in 2006. Sections of the building were renewed and repaired, with the clock mechanism being replaced and floodlighting installed to show off this wonderful piece of heritage in all its glory. Situated at the west end of High Street, it serves as a memorial to King Edward VII, a frequent visitor to the resort. It was erected in 1913, thanks to public subscription to the project. The original intention had been for a clock to celebrate his coronation, back in the summer of 1902, but insufficient funds were raised at the time. It was only after his death, in 1910, that the tower became a viable proposition once again as a further push for cash saw the public in a more generous mood. Even so, many regarded it as something of a white elephant and felt that the money could have been better spent elsewhere. The air raid shelters were a permanent reminder during the last war that even residents of a small coastal resort had to be on their guard, day and night. The mighty Teesside and Wearmouth shipyards and industrial plants were close enough for stray bombs to find their way to earth on our High Street or promenade.

Left: War Weapons Week was part of a special rallying call for Redcar's residents. In March 1941, Britain and her Commonwealth allies seemingly stood alone against the jackboot of fascism. The blitz on our homeland was well under way and we had become used to a regular diet of bombing raids. Rommel's Africa Korps was making headway in the desert and, out at sea, our convoys were having to dodge the aggressive U-boat packs. Price controls on food and rationing were making us tighten our belts and we realised that a communal effort was needed when the Minister of Labour, Ernest Bevin, sent out a message to mobilise over 100,000 women into filling vital jobs in industry and the auxiliary services. Cash donations, war bond purchase and salvage for recycling were all needed to top up the stock of weapons needed to fight the foe. Rallies such as this took place all over the land. Here Mayor Charles Harris JP addressed the crowd with stirring words. Sadly, he was to become a victim of the hostilities himself, later that year. On the night of 21st October, a social club, The Zetland in Coatham Road, received a direct hit during an air raid. Some 15 people, most of them local dignitaries, were killed. Mayor Harris was among them.

Above: When World War II began stockpiles existed of weapons that could be used to release chemicals and germs and the government was taking no chances. It was not just the men at the front who were under threat, civilians had become targets as never before. We knew all about aerial bombardment from newsreel footage of the German Condor squadrons that had aided Franco's cause in the Spanish Civil War and there was every reason to be concerned that a shell could contain anthrax just as much as high explosive. Officers of the Gas Identification Service were trained to detect evidence of any form of unconventional warfare and carried their own special equipment to help them in their task. As well as the usual gas masks, they were kitted out in special suits and boots to ensure that as little flesh as possible could be left exposed to potentially toxic substances. This group was on Linthorpe Road, Middlesbrough in c1941.

Top right: During the last war, Prime Minister Winston Churchill paid a number of whistle stop visits to places across the country that were vital to the war effort. Here he addressed a group of shipyard workers during his tour of the defence works and coastal fortifications in the northeast. His powerful oratory captured the crowd's attention. Churchill was a master at commanding the stage, whether it be on an election soapbox or when on his feet in the House of Commons. Although he sometimes employed ghostwriters to produce newspaper and magazine articles on his behalf, his wartime speeches were nearly all his own work. Moments of triumph or near tragedy seemed to inspire his greatest moments. On the day that war broke out he addressed Parliament by saying, 'We must not underrate the gravity of the task which lies before us or the temerity of the ordeal', but he will be best remembered for those that came later. On his first speech as prime minister he gave us the 'Blood, toil, tears and sweat' epic and followed this with 'We will fight them on the beaches' after the Dunkirk evacuation and his 'This was their finest hour' and 'Never in the field of human conflict', delivered either side of the Battle of Britain. Rather bizarrely, some of these speeches were delivered as radio repeats of Parliament by an impersonator, actor Norman Shelley.

Bottom right: 'Good old Winnie', as the prime minister affectionately became known in the early 1940s, visited the northeast on 31st July 1940, just as the Battle of Britain was well under way, largely in the skies over southern England. Churchill appeared with his trademark cigar clamped firmly between his teeth, fingers at the ready to raise the V for victory sign that he would employ later in the war as things took a turn for the better. He came to power on 10 May 1940 after it became apparent that the ineffective Neville Chamberlain had lost the confidence of both Parliament and the people. Already 65, Churchill was something of

© Imperial War Museum

a gamble as he belonged to the old order that had helped get us into the mess of another global conflict. However, he had been out of senior office during the 1930s and demonstrated a fierce opposition to German rearmament and the government's attempts at appeasement. He could rightly claim to have done his best in trying to face up to the Nazi threats. According to a popular myth, the Royal Navy issued a signal that read 'Winston is back'. Perhaps his greatest achievement was the way his stubborn belief in a final victory transmitted itself to the public. Some members of the cabinet wanted to sue for peace in 1940, but he would have none of it. He gave such lily livered colleagues his own V for victory sign.

© Imperial War Museum

The role of women in two world wars cannot be underestimated. In earlier times, men went off to do battle with Napoleon's troops, to the Crimea, to Afghanistan or South Africa in their many thousands, but the 20th century conflicts were something else. They departed in their millions, leaving behind factories, engineering works, farms and public transport vehicles without anyone to operate them. Step forward the fair sex. In 1914, women were not even allowed to vote for the people who drafted the legislation that took us into a war, but they stepped forward into the breach. They moved into areas of public, commercial and industrial life that had previously been out of bounds. Women's efforts in the war also embraced many different voluntary activities, in raising funds and providing materials for the forces. They were expected to swell the ranks of traditional jobs, such as nursing, but their contribution went much further. As the first world war continued to drain Britain's resources, both economically and in terms of manpower, the government began organising women's auxiliary military services to work in non-combatant roles and so release more men for fighting. Unprepared by prewar life for the conditions that many now faced, they bore it with great determination and no little humour. They tilled the fields and chopped down trees. Women

handled heavy engineering plant and served in factories geared up for the war effort. They got behind the wheel of ambulances, tractors and trams and even took on new skills, such as servicing aeroplanes for the Royal Flying Corps. Towards the end of the war, those with a particular determination put on uniforms and joined the Women's Auxiliary Army Corps or Women's Royal Air Force.

It was more of the same, but on a larger scale and with greater organisation, the second time round. When the balloon went up in 1939, there were already women's organisations officially in place. Stella, Lady Reading, founded her Women's Voluntary Service in 1938 and her members had already played their part in preparing the public for war on the home front with various civil defence training exercises. As men set off overseas, yet again women juggled home and family management with the demands of keeping the wheels of industry and food production turning. The Land Army was reformed in July 1939. Some 113,000 women, a third of all those employed in agricultural work, had done their bit in the service that was introduced in 1917, despite opposition from many farming communities. However, response was slow in World War II and only 7,000 initially joined up. It took government adverts that suggested the work was glamorous to swell the numbers. In fact, life on the land was tough and many land girls were placed on farms that lacked modern amenities of electricity or running water. Despite the publicity, the shortage of workers was so acute that, in 1943, women were actively discouraged from joining the armed forces and directed to farms or factories instead.

Those who opted for a uniform could enter any of the three armed forces. The Auxiliary Territorial Service was the army branch and, although some were destined for menial jobs as cleaners and domestics, others enjoyed the responsibility of driving trucks or becoming welders and electricians. Some were used to assist anti aircraft gunners by preparing shells, but they were not allowed to fire the actual weapons. Those in the Women's Auxiliary Air Force played a significant role as trackers during bombing missions. They also worked as mechanics and delivery pilots, flying Spitfires from factory to aerodrome. Members of the Women's Royal Naval Service also flew transport planes, as well as acting as clerks and wireless operators.

When peace was declared in 1945, there were 460,000 women in uniform and 6.5 million in civilian war work. Some of the latter had worked in dangerous conditions, such as the munitions factory at Newton Aycliffe, near Darlington. Most of the 17,000 workforce was female and they became known as the 'Aycliffe Angels'. Sadly some of them became real angels all too soon as this was dangerous work. Eight lost their lives in one particularly serious explosion. All these groups of women, whether in uniform or not, made up the army that Hitler forgot.

Above: Although preparing goodies for a party was traditionally mum's domain, it is poignant to note that it is difficult to spot an adult male in this shot of Middlesbrough's Garnet Street. As this was taken during the peace celebrations in 1919, then it is a sad possibility that some of the men who might have taken part were among the casualties of that terrible Great War. How many of these kiddies would grow up fatherless? In the meantime, the nation put a brave face on it and showed how glad it was that the cannons had stopped firing. The celebrations were tinged with hurt, as can be witnessed on the faces of this gathering that does not appear to be indulging in unbridled merriment. However, once the street party, held like many others in the back streets of the town centre, and beyond, got going then the children forgot their troubles for a while. Hopefully, the little lad standing on his chair did not topple headfirst into the road, but was able to resume his seat and enjoy the fruits of his mother's labours. Quite where the magnificent tea urn, resembling some regal Russian samovar, came from is not recorded. But it must have been someone's pride and joy and the envy of all the other housewives who turned out to mark the passing of the war to end all wars.

Right: Children from Brambles Infant School enjoyed a refreshing drink in September 1944. For them, the only real memories of their short lives were all related to the war. What sort of a world had they been born into, they must have thought, as they grew up in an environment of bombs falling from the sky, wrecked homes and town centres and fathers away on duty overseas. They had to get by on a restricted diet that only allowed them a few ounces of fresh meat and butter each week and their mothers had to make do and mend when it came to clothing youngsters who rapidly outgrew their shoes and clothes. At the start of the war, Operation Pied Piper was launched, evacuating thousands of children from the cities and places vulnerable to the air raids that the Spanish Civil War had taught us to fear. Train and bus loads of youngsters, labels around their necks and all clutching small suitcases, went into rural areas and smaller towns with their precious cargoes. They were billeted with families, who in the main welcomed them with open arms, but many were so homesick and their parents missed them so dreadfully that a large percentage made the return journey within months. However, the pressure to evacuate from the London area returned in the last 12 months of the war as V-1 and V-2 rockets were launched against the capital. Some youngsters came to Teesside and can be seen in this photograph.

Above: Endsleigh Drive is in Acklam, south of Middlesbrough and just off Levick Crescent. We are all well used to seeing pictures of VE and VJ parties that were held in the summer of 1945 as the war came to an end, but this celebration took place 12 months earlier. Although those later festivities were scenes of almost unbridled joy, there were earlier instances when we let our hair down to acknowledge turning points that occurred. In November 1942, British success during the North Africa campaign at El Alamein and the recapture of Tobruk led to the ringing of church bells all across our green and pleasant land. They had remained silent for three years as they were only to have been rung in the event of enemy invasion. Churchill later commented that, 'Before Alamein we never had a victory, after Alamein we never had a defeat'. It was a turning point and the next major one occurred on 6th June 1944 with the success of Operation Overlord. That date in history will forever be known as D-Day, the occasion when Allied troops landed on the Normandy beaches and started the long march to Paris and, eventually, Berlin. These children dressed up to celebrate the events of D-Day.

Corus - Men of Steel

The planned town of Middlesbrough, begun in 1830, was developed by a group of Quaker businessmen who held interests in south Durham coal mines and the Stockton and Darlington railway. Middlesbrough was to be a coal port for the outward shipment of coal and was planned to have a population of around 5,000. By the end of the 1830s, however, the local economy was slowing down. Ward Jackson had opened up West Hartlepool as a more efficient port for coal export and business at Middlesbrough was dwindling.

The owners looked for alternative business ventures, promoting pottery and persuading Henry Bolckow and John Vaughan to set up the town's first iron business. Bolckow was a German who had achieved success as a merchant in Newcastle. His brother-in-law, John Vaughan had worked in the iron industry in Wales, Staffordshire and at the Walker works in Newcastle. In 1839 they set up an iron and engineering works in the new town, employing Scots pig iron and Durham coke to make iron products for the marine and agricultural engineering trades. Rising prices and unstable supplies led the partners to establish their own blast furnaces at Witton Park in County Durham. This was not a great success and John Vaughan embarked on a search for significant seams of useable iron ore in Cleveland.

From the turn of the nineteenth century more systematic attempts were employed to extract and process the deposits of the various seams found on the moors and the coast. Following two years of investigations in East Cleveland, Vaughan and the mining engineer John Marley finally identified the 16 foot 'Main

Top left: *A Nineteenth century indenture, the legal foundation of iron and steel prosperity.* **Left:** *Nineteenth century accounting ledgers from Bell Bros. Part of the British Steel Collection at Teesside Archives.* **Below:** *'All done by human hands' (Lady Bell, At the Works, 1907). A group of workmen c.1900.*

Seam' at Upleatham in the Eston Hills. Not only was the seam wide, it was easily mined and close to the railway and the coast. For the next 25 years it served to make Middlesbrough the iron making capital of the world.

Bolckow and Vaughan built their first Cleveland blast furnaces at Eston and Middlesbrough in 1852. They were soon joined by a range of businessmen who would become household names, notably the Bell Brothers who had also been involved in the Walker plant in Newcastle, Bernard Samuelson, the Cochranes from Staffordshire, Gilkes, Wilson and Pease who formed the Teesside Ironworks and the engineer John Gjers, a Swede whose inventions and adaptations formed the basis of what has been called the Cleveland Blast Furnace Practice. Over the next 20 years blast furnaces appeared along the south side of the Tees from Stockton and Thornaby, through west and east Middlesbrough to Cargo Fleet, Eston and South Bank with outposts in Lackenby and Redcar. Only Bell Bros. developed a site north of the river, at Port Clarence.

Dated 1st January 1853.

Articles of Partnership

between

Messrs Bolckow & Vaughan

By the peak of pig iron production in 1873 there were almost 120 blast furnaces on the Tees. In the mid 1850s Teesside's output of 84,000 tons was equivalent to less than five percent of British production yet just five years later it had risen to 500,000 tons: in the boom year of 1873 it topped two million tons; one third of total British production of pig iron.

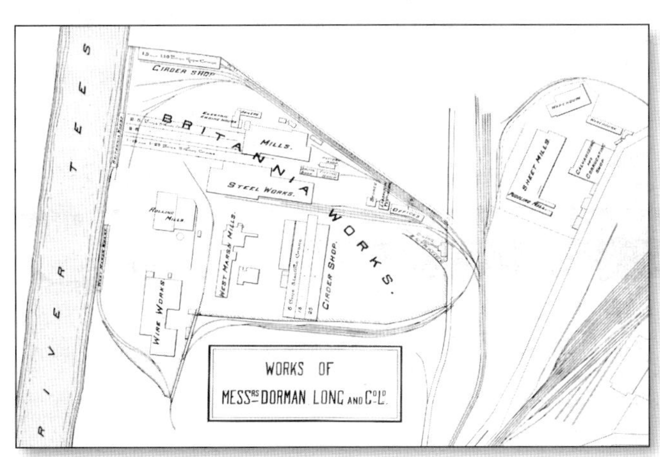

Top: ***Dixon's Dockyard 1921. Note Middlesbrough Ironworks to the right and Port Clarence in the foreground.*** ***Above:*** *An early partnership deed drawn up between Messrs Bolckow and Vaughan, pioneers of the Cleveland iron and steel industry, January 1853.* ***Left:*** *Dorman Long Britannia Works at the time of the merger with Bell Bros, 1901.*

Demand for iron and iron products was at its peak in this period. Railways were expanding around the world, demanding rails, boilers, engines and stations. Iron ships were replacing wooden vessels, construction called for more and more structural and ornamental ironwork whilst a range of industries, including mining and engineering, consumed more and more metal. The number of Teesside puddling furnaces (where pig iron was converted to malleable wrought iron or finished products) rose from under 200 in 1863 to around 750 ten years later, with 120 at Middlesbrough's new Britannia works alone. At the height of the boom Middlesbrough and district produced 600,000 tons of wrought iron, with over half that total to make rails for the world's railways, and 200,000 for shipbuilding.

But the boom did not last. The problem was the emergence of competition from steel. By the end of the 1870s steel had replaced iron almost entirely in the rail market and was beginning to challenge for the ship plate and boiler trade.

In the early 1870s, Bolckow Vaughan acquired a steel works in Manchester and interests in Spanish iron mines where the non-phosphorous ore had a higher metal content. By the end of the decade the company was producing acid steel by the Bessemer process. But it was also actively pursuing the means to use Cleveland ores and in 1879 recruited Sydney Thomas and his cousin Percy Gilchrist, who had solved the problem of phosphorous in pig iron. In essence, the Thomas-Gilchrist method involved the use of a base material (limestone or dolomite) to line the converter, giving it the name basic steel production – as opposed to acid production. Bolckow Vaughan went into full production in the early 1880s and was joined by the North Eastern Steel Co, a venture launched by Thomas and Gilchrist.

Steel making more generally, was driven by the new firm of Dorman Long, which set up in Middlesbrough in 1875. AJ Dorman was a works' manager at West Marsh Iron Company in Middlesbrough and Albert de Lande Long at Whitwell's in Stockton when they bought West Marsh to make iron bars and angles for the shipbuilding industry. They acquired Samuelson's Britannia Works in 1882 converting part of the plant to steel production utilising the Siemen Marten open hearth process. Dorman Long expanded rapidly, producing 100,000 tons of steel a year by 1890. As a result of experiments

to make open hearth steel using Cleveland ores, Dorman Long began to work closely with Bell Brothers of Port Clarence and in 1899 the firms merged. This was supplemented by the acquisition of the North Eastern Steel Company along with the Ayrton sheet mills and the Cleveland wire mills. By 1904 Dorman Long was producing 450,000 tons of steel.

Meanwhile, Dorman Long's main rival, Bolckow Vaughan, had developed steel production using the Basic Bessemer system at their huge Eston works and the South Durham Steel and Iron Company. By the turn of the century Bolckow Vaughan was worth almost £4,000,000 though it continued to suffer

Top left: *Tees-side Bridge and Engineering Works' Cricket Club, 1923. Captain C. Hugill.* ***Above:.*** *Cochrane's Foundry Foremen, c.1923.* ***Left:*** *Ingot Foundry, Clarence Works, c.1927.*

problems with its Bessemer converters, which pushed up prices and produced inferior products compared to continental imports. As a result it abandoned the Bessemer process and switched to basic open hearth production in 1911.

The South Durham Company was a new venture launched by the Hartlepool shipping tycoon, Sir Christopher Furness. He bought up firms in Stockton, Hartlepool and Tudhoe, County Durham to make steel and malleable iron. In the early 1900s he acquired the Cargo Fleet Iron Company to the east of Middlesbrough, which though obsolete offered an excellent site with access to the Tees and Cleveland ores. A new, modern, integrated site quickly challenged the dominance of Dorman Long and Bolckow Vaughan, producing around 125,000 tons of coke, pig iron and steel a year by the first world war. By 1914 the many firms which had formed the backbone of Cleveland's dominance of the iron trade had been substantially reduced to three giant iron and steel makers producing almost two million tons of steel annually.

Demand for iron and steel for the war effort bolstered the Cleveland industry, leading to further expansion, especially by Bolckow Vaughan which invested heavily in a new steel plant. Of particular significance for the future development of iron and steel making was the acquisition by Dorman Long of Walker's works at Redcar in 1915, as well as the Newport works in Middlesbrough two years later. It further extended production by converting the North Eastern Steel Company's works to open hearth production from 1919.

By the end of 1920 however, the industry was suffering from falling demand and prices along with increased foreign competition. The big three firms looked to protect themselves by the further acquisition of suppliers and by diversifying into new markets. Most successful was Dorman Long which rapidly expanded its bridge and construction work, securing the contract to build the prestigious Sydney Harbour Bridge. Other

Top left: *Casting pig iron as described by Lady Bell, Dorman Long and Co., c.1927.* ***Below:*** *Foundry, Clarence Works, c. 1927.*

orders followed, including the Tyne Bridge, Omdurman in the Sudan, Putney and a range of smaller structures. Dorman Long proved equally successful providing the steel for prestigious buildings, including the BBC's Bush House, the new ICI headquarters, the Strand Hotel and India House. At the same time South Durham moved into the production of steel pipes, aided by Talbot's invention of the hydro-carbon lining.

Bolckow Vaughan however had over stretched itself. It rarely ran at more than 50% production during the 1920s and began to accrue huge debts. In 1929 it merged with Dorman Long which now became the country's largest steel manufacturer, employing 33,000 workers. The merger brought Redpath Brown under Dorman's control which, together with the acquisition in 1930, of Tees-side Bridge and Engineering Works, consolidated its hold on UK steel construction. Although the firm went through a shaky period in the early 1930s, protective tariffs and covert government support allowed the firm to stabilise and recover. The Clarence and Newport works were closed, the former concentrating on chemicals, whilst a new coking plant (the largest in Europe) was constructed at the Cleveland works near Eston. The rolling of plates was concentrated at Redcar, a mill at Cleveland focused on light sections and bars whilst the remaining Middlesbrough plants specialised in heavy and semi-finished goods.

By the outbreak of the second world war Teesside iron and steel production had regained, to some extent, its position as the dominant producer of iron and heavy steels, with a particular emphasis on construction, structural engineering and bridge building. Ownership was concentrated in the hands of two major firms – Dorman Long and South Durham. Only Skinningrove Ironworks retained significant independence, largely by making use of cheap imported raw materials and focusing on specialist products, including 120 foot rails for London North Eastern Railways.

The interwar period had seen the growing importance of the works east of Middlesbrough in the production of the region's iron and steel. By 1939 more than two thirds of Dorman Long's iron, and three fifths of its steel, were produced east of the town.
That movement speeded up after the war as Dorman Long concentrated its production at Redcar and Lackenby. By the time of the Queen's coronation in 1953, almost

***Top left:** Limestone Quarrying at Parson's Green, c. 1927. **Centre:** A trademark steel bridge on the cover of a catalogue c.1930. **Right:** Ironstone miner leading his pony to the surface, c. 1927.*

three quarters of Dorman Longs' iron and steel were made at Redcar, the proportion rising further with the opening of the works at Lackenby.

Meanwhile the war had seen Teesside working at maximum capacity to meet the demand for munitions metals and structural steel, often in old or obsolete plant. There was limited cash for investment and a growing need for a national iron and steel strategy which led, in 1949, to the partial nationalisation of the industry. Although this was short lived, central control over the privatised sector was maintained through the Iron and Steel Board, which managed the future development of the industry. At South Durham new plant followed for the production of steel pipes at Stockton along with major investment in the integrated works at Greatham, south of Hartlepool, for the production of heavy plate. South of the Tees, Dorman Long modernised the South Bank Cleveland Works to undertake the preparation and coking processes and opened extensive new steel making furnaces at Lackenby which led to the closure of iron and steel making at Britannia Works and Cleveland Works. The Universal Beam Mill followed in 1958, allowing Dorman Long to compete successfully in the world market, even in the United States. Further investment at the Cleveland Works and Lackenby in additional furnaces, new technology, such as oxygen injection, and a range of finishing processes, such as light plate mills, continued the concentration of production in East Cleveland and led to the closure of the rolling mill at Britannia and the Acklam Works.

Dorman Long competed in both traditional markets and new ventures. It continued to be one of the world's leading bridge builders, with contracts including the Forth Road Bridge, the Tay Road Bridge and the Severn Bridge, which it built in partnership with Cleveland Bridge and Engineering Company and old rivals William Arrol. It played a significant role in the development of atomic power stations and made many of the country's electric pylons. However, despite these successes, in 1967 the Labour

Top left: *Young boys sorting ironstone, c. 1930.* ***Above:*** *Construction department, Dorman Long & Co.. The boy has just passed a white hot rivet to the engineer.* ***Below:*** *Plate shearing machine, Dorman Long & Co., Redcar, c.1930.*

government decided to re-nationalise the steel industry. The new British Steel Corporation was split into product divisions, with the remaining iron and steel works south of the river Tees, including Cleveland, Lackenby, Redcar, Britannia, Ayrton (collectively South Teesside Works) and Cargo Fleet, along with Hartlepool and Skinningrove becoming part of the General Steels Division. This change was accompanied by the move towards integrated multi-purpose coastal steel plants, with Teesside, South Wales and Scunthorpe at the centre of British Steel's future planning.

Extensive investment at Lackenby made it one of the largest integrated steel works in the western world, producing higher volumes – 4.5 million tonnes per annum - at considerably lower costs. These developments led to the closure of older open hearth plants at Redcar, Cargo Fleet, Lackenby and Skinningrove and the further concentration of ironmaking at Lackenby/Redcar. The concentration of production in East Cleveland was facilitated by improved deep water facilities at the mouth of the Tees which aided the importation of large quantities of cheap iron ore – required by the virtual exhaustion of the Cleveland fields, the last mine closing in 1964. Further efficiencies came from technological change, especially the introduction of the Basic Oxygen Plant which reduced the time required for each steel making cycle from ten hours to 40 minutes. Overall Teesside remained a dominant player in British iron and steel production, making around an eighth of the national output, with a concentration on the heavy types of material for which the region was famous, especially beams, heavy plates and bars for the engineering, shipbuilding and gas and oil industries.

In 1972 the government announced that it would invest £1,000 million in a new integrated plant at Redcar capable of producing 12 million tons per annum. Work began on the site in 1974 and continued through to the end of the decade with the Redcar Number 1 blast furnace being lit in November 1979.

Unfortunately a world steel market recession necessitated a major re-think of the 1972 plan. The plan for a second blast furnace at Redcar was shelved, rolling mill capacity had to be reduced and considerable job losses followed. The need to reline the one blast furnace at Redcar jeopardised the future of Redcar/South Teesside as a continuous strip mill.

Throughout the 1970s British Steel shed 21,000 jobs in the North East, leaving a workforce of just 7,000 in South Tees a

Top left: *Dorman Long's Sydney Harbour Bridge at night, soon after its opening in 1932.* ***Above right:*** *India House, Aldwych during construction. The building contained 'over 1,000 tons of British Steel, manufactured and fabricated by Dorman Long & Co.' c.1930.* ***Right:*** *'In the glare of the furnace' from Middlesbrough Pictorial-Industrial (1934) Middlesbrough: Press Publications Ltd [TA].*

decade later. World demand picked up in the mid-1980s and British Steel moved back into profit, leading both the management and the Conservative government to push for privatisation.

Following the British Steel Act of 1988 the Corporation and its Teesside works became part of British Steel Limited, which in 1999 merged with the Dutch company Koninklijke Hoogovens to form Corus.

In 2003, after reviewing its steelmaking strategy, Corus decided that the steel made at the Teesside plant was surplus to requirements and that in order for the Teesside plant to survive another outlet for its steel had to be found. This was the start of the unique 'consortium' agreement that was brokered between four international steel businesses and Corus. The consortium members who have made a long term commitment to the Teesside works are: Dongkuk Steel of South Korea, Duferco of Switzerland, APM of Mexico and Italian company Marcegaglia.

Thanks to the depth of knowledge, determination to succeed and pride in steelmaking on Teesside, in 2004 the consortium members signed a landmark agreement with Corus' Teesside Cast Products to supply steel to them for the next ten years. The consortium and Corus continue to invest in the steel works and all parties hope the agreement will be extended long beyond the original ten years.

Today, with 1,800 employees and the support of hundreds of contractors, Corus on Teesside makes over 3million tonnes of steel annually. That sophisticated steel is used for a wide range of things including ships, white goods, bridges, buildings, car parts...the list is endless.

In addition to steelmaking, Corus also has other steel related operations on Teesside: it operates a beam mill, which takes the steel made on Teesside and Scunthorpe and rolls it into a range of beams and columns predominantly for use in the construction sector. The company also has three mills at Hartlepool, which manufacture large diameter tubes for use in the oil, gas and construction industry.

Corus Northern Engineering Services provides consulting services; in addition there are also people working at a corporate and divisional level.

Teesside is also home to the Corus Teesside Technology Centre. The Centre provides technology input to Corus businesses to improve product quality and to maximise efficiency. With an international reputation the Teesside Technology Centre also provides its services to other companies from both the UK and worldwide.

There have been many changes in the Corus history but one thing remains constant. Corus is committed to making a significant contribution to the wealth and wellbeing of the region and its people. It is passionate about steel, and is proud to build on the accomplishments of the men and women who over many years have contributed to the industry.

In 2007 Corus became part of the multi-national Tata Steel Group.

Top: *Cochrane's Wharf, c.1936.* ***Below:*** *Redcar Blast Furnace Control Room, 2007.*

SPORTING LIFE

Ayresome Park was Middlesbrough's home from 1903 until 1995, when it relocated to the Riverside Stadium. It was built on Paradise Field, next to the old stadium where Middlesbrough Ironopolis FC played a season in the Football League in 1893-94. The highest attendance was recorded for the game against Newcastle United on 27 December 1949 when 53,802 spectators came through

the turnstiles. Apart from a brief period in the 1920s, the club played in the first division until the mid 1950s when it was relegated. Middlesbrough stayed outside the top flight until gaining promotion in 1974. It was back in the doldrums in the 1980s and bounced up and down between the top two divisions in the 1990s before settling back into the big time in 1998. The ground was honoured during the 1966 World Cup by being chosen to host some of the group stage matches, including the famous North Korean victory over mighty Italy. This more humble match in the photograph was played in a fixture from the mid 1960s against Huddersfield Town. The left winger sliding the ball into the back of the net was a young Derrick Downing, who was playing only his third first team match for the club. He had been plucked from non league soccer with Frickley Athletic, the West Yorkshire colliery side, in 1965. He played nearly 200 games before moving to Orient in 1972.

Right and below: The late 1940s were not just the baby boom years. After the second world war, attendances at public sporting events rocketed. People had been deprived of such top class entertainment for more than six years and queues at cricket grounds and soccer stadiums stretched around the block. It was not uncommon for spectators to be in place in their seats or on the terraces an hour before the start and for turnstiles to be closed not long after. Although the initial surge was over by the 1949-50 football season, Ayresome Park could still boast large attendances. It was on 27th December 1949 when the ground record was set as over 53,000 made their way through the gates to watch the side managed by David Jack play host to its rival, Newcastle United. During this period, Andy Donaldson became the club's first five figure transfer when he signed from the St James Park club. Middlesbrough was going through one of its more successful phases, spending some 25 years in the top flight before being relegated in 1954. George Hardwick skippered the side pictured here. He was one of our most famous players, but like so many of his era, his playing career was interrupted by the war. Hardwick, a local lad from Saltburn, played for the national side on 13 occasions. The goalkeeper, Italian born Rolando

Ugolini, made over 300 appearances for Middlesbrough, but the most charismatic player we had at the time must be the one and only Wilfrid James Mannion. Wilf was born in South Bank in 1918 and was spotted playing for St Peters in the local league. He signed professional forms in 1936 and made his first team

debut in 1937 against Portsmouth. His silky skills as an inside forward soon attracted rave reviews and he must have been on the verge of making the national side when war broke out not long after his 21st birthday. He saw active service with the Green Howards and was one of those who made it back safely from Dunkirk. During the war, footballers were given some time off to play in morale boosting games and Mannion played several times for England and gave displays that had spectators marvelling at his wizardry. After being demobbed, he returned to Ayresome Park to take up the threads of an interrupted career. A first full cap was awarded in May 1947 for the match against Northern Ireland. The 'golden boy', as the papers had dubbed him, did not disappoint. He scored a hat trick. Wilf played 26 times for his country, a figure that he could have doubled but for the war. After leaving Middlesbrough in 1954, he had a short spell at Hull City. He died in 2000, but lives on in the form of the statue outside the Riverside that commemorates his contribution to the club's history

Left: Middlesbrough FC 1949-50
Back row, R. Robinson, W. Linacre, W. Whitaker, R. Ugolini, P. McKennan, J Gordon. Front row, A. McCrae, P. Desmond, G. Hardwick, W. Mannion, H. Bell.

Above: There was only one Wor Jackie and that was Milburn, but this Jackie, a son of Ashington and cousin of Newcastle's legendary centre forward, was a major force in soccer for some 40 years. Raising a glass to Middlesbrough's triumphant return to the first division, Jack Charlton spent a successful four years as manger at Ayresome Park. He took charge at the end of the 1972-73 season and galvanised the side into achieving promotion in his first full year in charge. He was one of those able to make the transition from top flight football as a player to a similar status in management. Elder brother of the more gifted Bobby, the long serving Manchester United star, Jack initially followed a more pedestrian career as a centre half with Leeds United. It was not until Don Revie arrived as manager that the club's fortunes and those of its players changed for the better. Promotion to Division One meant playing in more high profile games and Jack won his first England cap in the month before his 30th birthday and went on to play in 35 internationals, including that marvellous World Cup winning day in 1966. After Middlesbrough, Jack managed Sheffield Wednesday before returning briefly to Ayresome Park and then spent a year at Newcastle before landing the job in 1985 that won him managerial fame as boss of the Republic of Ireland. After a decade in charge, during which time he had helped Ireland change from footballing minnows to international somebodies, Jack picked up his beloved fishing rod and left.

Below: During the 1960s, crowds came to soccer and cricket matches that were organised for various charities. These knockabouts between stars of screen, stage and music against more established players, became quite popular for a while. People came to see the likes of Freddie Garrity, without his Dreamers, jumping around a football field. Ageing players donned their boots again and turned out against some of the strangest sides that they had ever faced and the fans, particularly younger ones, cheered wildly. This match between a Showbiz XI and an All Stars XI was held at Clairville Stadium on 4 November 1966. This was just a few months after England had won its only trophy of any significance when Bobby Moore lifted the World Cup and soccer's popularity grew on the back of that success. The game was played to raise funds for the village of Aberfan where a fortnight earlier a slagheap had been washed down in heavy rain and engulfed the primary school below, killing 144 people of whom 116 were children. Clairville Stadium was opened by the Duke of Edinburgh in 1963 as a cinder track and cycle velodrome and was formerly known as the Cleveland County Stadium. The running track was upgraded in the mid 1970s.

Right: Des McPartland made a flying save to thwart the Bury attack in this action photo taken in 1966. Neville Chapman, the right fullback, was keeping a watchful eye in case the keeper spilled the ball. McPartland never held down a regular place, playing just 35 times in three years before being transferred to Carlisle United. Chapman's career at Ayresome was similarly spasmodic, playing for the first team on just 53 occasions in a six year spell before heading inland along the Tees to Darlington in 1967. Although this was World Cup year and Middlesbrough was proud to host some of the group stage matches, the times were not good for the club. Although the opponents on this day had a poor season, they at least managed to miss relegation. Not so for our boys as they ended two points below Bury and suffered the ignominy of dropping into Division Three. Manager Raich Carter, who never achieved the heights behind a desk that he did on the playing field, was sacked before the end of the season as the board of directors saw the writing on the wall. New boss Stan Anderson could not prevent the drop, but he steered the club out of Division Three the following season. He was to stay for over six years, but was unable to get Middlesbrough back into the top division that it left in 1954.

Middlesbrough speedway had its home at Cleveland Park, which was opened to the public May 1928, when the very first greyhound meeting took place. Later that year on 23rd August 1928 the inaugural dirt track meeting was staged as 'The Stockton Handicap'. Ladies were allowed in for free and it is estimated that a bumper crowd of up to 15,000 spectators watched proceedings.

The third meeting was to feature local farmers daughter Eva Asquith (pictured), a well know grass track rider from Bedale. Riding a Velocete she made a poor start in her first race but improved to finish second in her next race.

After a season of open meetings in 1928, Middlesbrough joined the English Dirt Track Northern League for the 1929 season. After several years of open meetings, Middlesbrough's first taste of success came as Northern League Champions in 1946. A record crowd at Cleveland Park occurred in 1948 when almost 16,000 spectators watched the opening night fixture against Sheffield 'Tigers'. However after finishing third in the League the gates were closed again.

Speedway returned to Middlesbrough on a regular occurance after a 13 year absence under the control of

promoter Reg Fearman, in April 1961. This continued for a four year period until the team transferred to Halifax.

Eric Boothroyd, who went on to captain Halifax, had a speedway career spanning four decades as a successful rider and promoter and enjoyed three seasons at Middlesbrough between 1961 – 1963. He obtained a promoters licence in 1966 and fought to gain permission against the authorities to stage open licence meetings at Cleveland Park. He staged 10 meetings but after an indifferent response, the track was closed again in July when he bowed out in a match against a Clive Hitch Select team.

Far left: Early 1960s as Middlesbrough captain Eric Boothroyd leads team mate Freddie Greenwell at Cleveland Park, Middlesbrough.

Above: Middlesbrough team photograph 1961. From left to right: Maurice Morley (team manager), Eric Boothroyd, Don Wilkinson, Rik France, Vic Lonsdale, Tommy Roper, Geoff Pymer, captain (on bike), Freddie Greenwell (kneeling).

Left: Middlesbrough Bears legend Frank Hodgson, captain from 1946-48.

'Now then, just listen to me for a minute, young man.' He was irascible, forthright and self opinionated, but he was also a good footballer, excellent manager and upholder of professional behaviour both on the field and off it. He was, Brian Clough. As a leader of men, he did not suffer fools gladly, but was fiercely loyal to his friends and supporters.

'Cloughie' was born at 11 Valley Road, Grove Hill, Middlesbrough on 21st March 1935, the fifth of eight children. He was proud of his close family and its working class roots. A code of ethics he learned at his mother's apron strings would stay with him throughout his life. As a child, he stood on the terraces and thrilled at the skills of Wilf Mannion, one of Middlesbrough's golden boys of the immediate postwar era. His own playing ability earned him a place in the Billingham Synthonia side when he was just a young teenager, but his home town club snapped up his signature on professional terms after he returned from national service duties in 1955. He forced his way into the first team and was an immediate sensation as a centre forward, scoring 40 times in 1956-57. In all, he notched 203 goals in 222 first team games, a phenomenal return at any level, never mind the professional game. Surprisingly, he won just two England caps in 1959 before moving to Sunderland, where he continued to find the back of the net on a regular basis. His career was cut short by a serious knee injury on Boxing Day 1962. He tried to make a comeback, but had to admit defeat and retired from playing.

At the ender age of 30 he was given the manager's job at Hartlepool United, with Peter Taylor as his assistant. This was to be the start of a long and successful partnership. After helping the northeast side achieve healthy results, the duo moved to Derby County in 1967. The Baseball Ground team was languishing in the lower reaches of Division Two and Clough rattled a few cages by clearing out substandard players and other staff. He brought in new faces, but the master stroke was the signing of Dave Mackay. He was a veteran, but one with a powerful personality who helped drive Derby back into Division One. The side got there by playing good soccer, but without the nasty tactics that some of Clough's managerial colleagues promoted in their players. That attitude of hard but fair play would epitomise his sides throughout the rest of his career. Derby won the league title

in 1972. By then, Clough had become well known for his controversial statements about other managers and officialdom. In 1973 he and Taylor left the Baseball Ground after falling out with the chairman and took over at Brighton.

After a year on the south coast, Clough split with Taylor and succeeded Don Revie at Leeds United, a job that lasted just 44 days. Even Brian Clough could not overcome the resentment that greeted his move to Elland Road.

Before long, Nottingham Forest had him back at the reins. He immediately laid plans for a return to Division One and gained promotion 18 months later. By then, Taylor was back as his second in command. They went from strength to strength, winning the championship in that first season back in the top flight. More was to follow. In 1979 Clough made Trevor Francis the country's first £1 million signing and Forest went on to win the European Cup that year and retain it in 1980. Although his team continued to play good

football, the big city clubs and the turnovers they had meant that the real glory days would be limited for smaller ones. He retired in 1993, by which time he had lost his edge and Forest was about to be relegated.
Brian Clough was always one for speaking his mind. As a committed socialist, he was supportive of the downtrodden. He took a keen interest in his family and was thrilled when son, Nigel, won the first of 14 England caps in 1989. This made the Cloughs father and son England internationals, matching the Easthams and the later Lampards. He died in 2004 and a bronze statue in Albert Park was later erected in his memory. It shows him as a young player on his way to training.

Above: The thunder of hooves, as they head for the winning post in the last few yards of the final furlong, is an exciting sound, guaranteed to get the crowd roaring itself hoarse, if you will pardon the pun. It was a close call in the finish of this 1962 race and punters waited anxiously for the judges' verdict before heading off to claim their winnings or tear up their tickets in disgust. Bookmakers signalled the odds on those in the top three places by waving their arms and tapping their shoulders in their own particular brand of sign language known as 'tic-tac'. The inaugural meeting at Redcar Racecourse took place in August 1872. Admission to the course was set at 2d (1p), with a king's ransom of 6s (30p) being charged to those wealthy enough to afford seats in the grandstand. Before the racecourse opened, horse racing was frequently held on the sands at Coatham during the early 19th century. Ropes were used to mark out the equivalent of the track and the officials were sited in rather incongruous spots. The steward stood on the back of a cart and the judges took up position in a bathing machine. Redcar has seen all the top jockeys and trainers, from Fred Archer to Frankie Dettori and Noel Murless to Michael Stoute.

EVENTS & OCCASIONS

The 1925 King and Queen of Redcar Carnival paused outside Jack Longstaff's in Marske High Street to pose for a moment and enjoy their few hours of fame. It was everyone's ambition to ride the float as the chosen ones each year, but it was an honour that only came to a privileged few. Naturally, every mother felt that her son or daughter deserved the right to be at the head of the parade, but that was only

natural. Just as understandable was the secret jealousy felt by those parents whose delightful offspring had been rejected. They smiled their approval and uttered their praise though gritted teeth. Such festivals, carnivals and procession were an important part of our lives in the first half of the last century. These events demonstrated a community spirit and helped celebrate a village or town's achievements. They were also jolly occasions as the parades wound their way through the streets and invariably ended up with an afternoon and evening of dancing, entertainment and all the fun of the fair. Some of the processions had a religious significance. The annual Whit walk was a prime example. Parading in a new set of clothes and collecting cash from assorted uncles and aunts was a feature of life in those days. Marske has a peculiar claim to fame. Its former aerodrome inspired WE Johns to write his Biggles books.

Above: Although they did not realise it at the time, the crowds lining Redcar's High Street were preparing for the great marching off ceremonies that would take place just over a year later when our boys went off to France full of pride and optimism. On 29th July 1913, some 2,500 Territorials of the York and Durham Brigade paraded in a show of strength that demonstrated that Britain was still a mighty force to be reckoned with on the world stage. At that time, there were rumblings across the globe, with trouble in the Balkans and neighbouring areas as Turkey, Serbia, Macedonia, Greece and Bulgaria all had territorial disputes that would also bring Romania and Montegran armies onto the battlefield. Political commentators also noted that Germany had considerably increased its army and it was time for Britain to put on a public display of might. Colonel JE Bush became the Brigade's first commander in 1911. It was renumbered as 150 Brigade, 50th Division in 1915. As the men marched through Redcar, how many of them imagined what would be facing them over the next few years? The arms race accelerated in the early spring of 1914 as Austria-Hungary gave precedence in its budget to armaments, Russia quadrupled its army and the Kaiser commissioned new warships. Then came the assassination of Archduke Franz Ferdinand in June and Europe was soon ablaze.

Below: At the eleventh hour on the eleventh day of the eleventh month each year we still remember those who gave their lives so that we could live in peace. Although there were memorials in some parks, churchyards and town centres to honour those who had fallen in such conflicts as the Afghan Wars and the Boer Wars of the previous century, nothing compared to the massive, collective display of appreciation that took place after the first world war. The immensity of the loss of life touched every family in the land and everywhere, from the smallest village to the largest city, a war memorial was erected on which the names were etched of those who had made the ultimate sacrifice. Middlesbrough's War Memorial was unveiled on 11th November 1922 and we can get an idea of the thousands who turned up to honour fallen comrades from the density of the crowd in the photograph. In July 1919, a day was set aside as Peace Day and was intended to be a quiet occasion, marked by the unveiling of the Cenotaph in London. However, such was the attendance and feeling across the country, that plans were soon afoot to introduce a similar memorial in each town. When, in November, King George V proclaimed that a two minute silence should be observed and 'all locomotion should cease so that, in perfect stillness, the thoughts of everyone may be concentrated on reverent remembrance of the glorious dead', the noble tradition was established.

Left: During the last war there occasions when the morale of the nation needed bolstering. Constant aerial bombardment in the early 1940s, plus the tightening of the belts enforced by stringent rationing, meant that not everyone was happy with his lot. To dispel grumbles, the government embarked on a series of displays that were meant to reassure the population and promote its continued support for the war effort. Tanks trundled across the country and were parked up in town squares as a symbol of military might. Spitfires were wheeled into view and acted as a reminder of the brave actions of our pilots in the Battle of Britain. Fund raising by contribution or the purchase of war bonds and certificates was encouraged and locals were asked to stump up cash to sponsor a plane, tank or ship that they could relate to and call their own. Thermometers illustrating the amount of money donated by residents were strapped to churches and town halls and competition between neighbouring districts was encouraged. This field gun was parked in front of Middlesbrough Town Hall. This symbol of the town's incorporation as a borough in 1853 was built between 1883 and 1887. Its façade was decorated with a number of statues that include St George, Justice and figures that represent the arts and the town's maritime traditions.

AJESTIE
HEY

Left: Some of the floral lettering seems to have come detached in this message on Middlesbrough Town Hall that should have read 'Majesties – Long May They Reign'. The garlands and decorations bedecked the imposing building as part of the celebrations for the silver jubilee. The photograph was taken on 6th May 1935, marking 25 years on the throne for King George V. Sadly, his reign had not much longer to run as within a year he was gone. The Town Hall was opened by his father, later Edward VII, who officiated in his then role as Prince of Wales on 23rd January 1889, accompanied by his wife, Alexandra. The building was given Grade II listed status in 1963 and still retains many of its original features, being an impressive headquarters for local government in municipal buildings that vaguely resemble the Houses of Parliament. The modern town centre is very different from the original town conceived by Joseph Pease in 1829. The early town, now known as St Hilda's, after the parish church, was focused on a market square, but the coming of the railway led to growth to the south, leaving the old town isolated between river and railway. Since its earliest days, the Town Hall has been the home of entertainment in Middlesbrough. Many famous names from the past have appeared, including Harry Lauder, Gracie Fields, Johann Strauss and Richard Tauber. Oscar, the building's resident ghost, also puts in occasional appearances.

Above: 'Up with the gun and down with the Hun' is hardly the sort of poetry that Wilfrid Owen wrote in the trenches in 1917-18 and is more in keeping with the jingoistic doggerel that Jessie Pope submitted to popular newspapers such as the Daily Mail at that time. However, the ordinary man in the street probably identified more easily with such simply expressed sentiment than anything from 'Anthem for Doomed Youth', even if its content was more thought provoking and stylish. Certainly, the powers that be had little time for the likes of Owen and Sassoon, even if they had been aware of their poetry. They would have seen their outpourings as treasonable utterances rather than cries from the heart. At home, visits by the royal family were organised in an attempt to maintain morale and acknowledge the work being done by civilians in supporting the war effort. King George V and Queen Mary, she as ever resplendent in the remarkable headgear she always favoured, came to Teesside on Thursday, 14th June 1917 to inspect the shipyards and munitions factories.

Below: The University of Teesside boasts a student population of over 20,000. Its entrance is at the site of the old Constantine building, fronted by the Waterhouse clock tower. The building of a main higher education centre to replace the 1844 Mechanics' Institute was a long time in coming as the raising of the appropriate funding was a stumbling block. Progress towards this new provision was slow and only really kickstarted by a generous donation of £40,000 made in 1916 by the philanthropic shipping magnate, Joseph Constantine. Even then, with a war and its aftermath to be considered, it took until 1922 before a governing council was even formed. The Constantine family doubled the amount of the original gift in 1924 and, at long last, GR Dawbam, a London architect, was commissioned in March 1926. Building work began the following year and the first students enrolled in September 1929. The formal dedication of the new technical college had to wait until 2nd July 1930. Here the mayor and other dignitaries and learned fellows made their way towards the dais where the Prince of Wales, the future Edward VIII, seen here doffing his hat, performed the opening ceremony. Although not yet a university, Constantine Technical College offered some degree courses that were validated by the University of London. It achieved polytechnic status in 1969, before being elevated to full university ranking in 1992.

Right: The smart young things showed off their knees in short dresses born of the flapper era when women went in for a fashion style that horrified the older generation. Before the first world war, it was largely floor length hemlines and high collars, but women's liberation in the voting booths went hand in glove with a greater freedom in clothing styles. Brighter colours and patterns accompanied the new feminine look, as did shorter hairstyles and a desire to be seen out and about, rather than chained to the kitchen sink. The young women taking pole position in this crowd in 1930 acted a little like movie and pop music fans of today as they craned their necks for a better view of the celebrity who was due to appear shortly. However, it was not Douglas Fairbanks or Whispering Jack Smith who was coming to call. It was our very own Prince of Wales. Edward, heir to the throne as the eldest son of George V, represented his father on many official visits in the years leading up to his brief reign as Edward VIII. In the 1920s he courted popularity by displaying a particular interest in the unfortunate plight of those on the poverty line. His flamboyant air and good looks were attractive to the opposite sex and some women in the crowds who turned out to see him were close to swooning as he made his entrance.

Below: The Prince of Wales doffed his hat to the cheering crowd that greeted him on his visit to the Dorman Long Britannia Steel Works on 2nd July 1930. The company was, perhaps, the country's chief bridge builder of its time. It was founded in 1875 when Arthur Dorman and Albert de Lande Long leased blast furnaces from the West Marsh Iron Company in order to manufacture bars and angles used in shipbuilding. The firm rapidly grew as the order books filled and by the first world war had become a major industrial force on Teesside. Takeovers and amalgamations of other companies helped further expansion after the war and this was particularly enhanced when important rivals such as Bell Brothers and Bolckow and Vaughan came under the Dorman Long umbrella. Its 1929 Tyne Bridge won a host of admirers for its design and level of workmanship. Prince Edward's visit reflected the level to which the company had risen in the nation's list of important industries. The iconic Sydney Harbour Bridge was built here, as was the impressive single span Newport Lifting Bridge that was opened by the Prince's brother, the Duke of York in February 1934. The Dorman Museum next to Albert Park was presented to the town by the co-founder in 1904 in memory of his son, George, who died of fever while on service in South Africa during the Boer War.

The tramp of marching boots sounded along Coatham Road in 1930 as members of the armed forces led the way in the procession that celebrated Mayor's Day in Redcar. A show of force was thought to be good for public morale at a time when the northeast was feeling the pinch of the depression more than most. It was meant to remind everybody that Britain was still a great power with influence across the world. After all, much of the globe was still painted red as a sign that the sun would never set on our Empire. In less than two decades that would all change. Our international influence would be diminished and our overseas colonies and dominions would commence snapping the bonds that held them to the so-called mother land. People on the street knew little of what was happening abroad, even if they had heard something of a half naked chap called Ghandi. They also knew a tiny bit about some funny little German with a daft moustache, but that is another story. In the meantime, Teessiders were more interested in what was happening in the mines and shipyards that provided them with the wherewithal to feed their families. The number of jobs was falling and every family began to feel the pinch as unemployment in Britain passed the million mark. That figure would treble over the next few years.

CAPERN'S
BIRD SEEDS
CAPERN'S
MELOX

Below: The entrance to Mineral Street was guarded by two make believe sentries in May 1937. Nearby, a trio of smartly kitted out youngsters waited their turn to join in the celebrations for the coronation of King George VI. Six months earlier, the nation had been expecting that this day would see Edward VIII ceremonially enthroned as our monarch, but that was before the abdication crisis reached its conclusion as he stood down from his royal duty and went into exile with the twice divorced American socialite, Wallis Simpson. His brother, Albert Frederick Arthur George, or Bertie to his family, stepped into the breach and was crowned on the very day originally set aside for the man who had, by then, disappeared to France. The new king had neither expected nor wanted the throne. He was a diffident, even painfully shy, figure who battled throughout his life with a nervous stammer. The general public was split in its opinion over the abdication, but unanimous in its support of George VI, recognising that he had to reunite his family and heal the divisions caused by his brother. Consequently, the bunting flew, the flags were unfurled and banners were hung from windows, all proclaiming 'God save the King'. He was to serve his country well for a quarter of a century.

Right: Just for a moment it looked as if we had strayed into London and were within shouting distance of the Bow Bells as we look at the central character in this group. She was no pearly queen, but one of our own gemstones enjoying herself with her pals as they celebrated the Middlesbrough Deanery Pageant in 1937. They did well to put on such happy faces as they were rattling their charity collection tins on a typically soggy northeastern day. Still, they did not seem to mind the rain and who would if you were having fun? Pageants and processions were very popular either side of the last war and individual churches held their own, just as much as towns, villages and other societies. Hardly a weekend seemed to go by without some group of gaily decorated floats trundling by, one of which was topped off by a pretty girl who was Queen of something or other. Let us hope that those cocoa tins got filled with plenty of tanners that made their way to the coffers of the noble cause which the young women were supporting.

Left: During War Weapons Week, held in Redcar in 1941, local bigwigs and senior members of the armed forces addressed crowds and urged them to support the war effort. Unlike other war charities, no money was paid to a named cause. Instead, residents in every town were asked to save money in a variety of government accounts. They were issued with bonds and certificates that had a twofold aim. They would encourage savings that the Treasury could draw upon as well as providing people with a sense of satisfaction that they were 'doing their bit'. Other gimmicks to promote the idea including getting the service of celebrities who would attract attention to the cause. Jack Warner lent his voice to the campaign and helped swell the Redcar crowds. In later years, he would become a much loved character on television in the long running 'Dixon of Dock Green' series. But, he was a household name long before the time of the gogglebox. He was born Horace Waters in London in 1896 and, after service as a pilot in the 1914-18 War, he trod the boards as part of a comedy double act. His sisters, Elsie and Doris, kept the family name and established themselves as a formidable variety turn, often using the alter egos of Gert and Daisy. Warner moved into straight acting and landed a number of leading roles in the 1930s, but his career really took off in the 1940s, culminating in the TV role that ran from 1955 for over 20 years. 'Evening all.'

SHOPPING SPREE

Lower East Street runs away from the junction of Cleveland Street and Durham Street towards part of the old dockland. Wiseman's was obviously a forerunner of the Army and Navy stores we know today and it sold similar goods that were just right for heavy duty wear. Men can be seen hunting through the items on display on the street stalls that would provide lengthy service as work trousers, overalls or hardy jackets as they performed their jobs on the ships or at the yards down by the river. The Britannia Hotel in the background was a popular drop in place for men who fancied a pint after work. Pubs in the early 20th century were a far cry from those experienced today. They were basically drinking dens where men could meet, talk, play games and argue the toss in an almost exclusively male environment. Drinkers could escape from the humdrum existence at work or at home and take it easy in the companionship of other men. There was a sad corollary for some as they stayed too long and spent too much, to the detriment of their families waiting for the breadwinner to return home in a sorry state.

ARMY GOODS Of Every Description
THIS IS WISEMAN'S The Shop FOR GOOD BOOT
SEAMEN
OUTFITTE
LARGE STOCKS AT LOWEST POSSIBLE PRICES.
TRY WISEMAN FOR ARMY GOOD Of Every Descrip
THIS IS WISEMAN'S THE WORKING MANS FRIEND.

Right: We were definitely cooking with gas in this 1938 view of the showroom at 68 High Street, Redcar. These appliances now belong in a museum or could be used to fit out a model home from the interwar years. Yet, although they look laughably outmoded to our eyes, these were part of state of the art technology 60 years ago. No doubt our great-grandchildren will mock the Dyson cleaner, the split level hob and the dual core computer processor in years to come. We have to put things into perspective. When these gas stoves, boilers and fridges were on the market, many still cooked on open ranges, washed clothes in a dolly tub and kept food in the larder. Some houses and streets still had gas lighting as electricity had not reached everywhere. Our relationship with gas goes back over 200 years. William Murdoch, a Scottish engineer who moved to Redruth, Cornwall in the late 18th century, was the first to install gas lighting in a house. The Valor gas cookers and Acme washers that we might recall from our parents' homes were developments from his pioneering work. Which of us can forget the joy of getting a gas poker to use to light the fire, instead of that dreadful struggle with screwed up newspaper and sticks?

Left: At your service for cycles, radios and furniture was Arthur Jackson's premises at 105 High Street and other neighbouring outlets that formed part of the Redcar business. There was a sale on and members of the family business and co-workers posed for this promotional shot in 1938. As far as home entertainment went, radio was the main medium. We listened to gramophone records on wind up machines that needed new needles every few plays, but it was the BBC coming over the airwaves that made our evenings enjoyable. The wireless was the focal point in any living room. Throughout that decade, as 'the Beeb' flourished and reached out to more and more people across the nation, eminent writers, actors and performers were heard in plays, discussions, sports and variety programmes. Among the most popular ones were comedy shows like 'ITMA' and 'Comedy Bandwaggon'. Those with musical interests enjoyed the sounds of the BBC Dance Orchestra, led by Henry Hall. The flavour of this prewar image is furthered by fashion styles and the car model, but it is the delivery bicycle that might catch some eyes. Most shops had a boy who would pedal off down the road, his basket filled with goods or produce that a customer had ordered, and make a home delivery. Whistling as he went, like Granville from 'Open all hours', the lad went through the whole hit parade of popular songs.

Above: ME Watts' Market Café on Dacre Street also doubled as a lodging house, offering bed and breakfast for travelling salesmen and sailors waiting for their next berth. It was situated in the part of Middlesbrough that was laid out in the grid-iron pattern around a market square devised by Joseph Pease in the early days of the town. The proprietor was photographed outside her business in c1920. We can only wonder where the male of the household might have been, but there is a sad possibility that he was one of those who did not return from serving king and country during the Great War. What was going through the minds of these women as they gazed out from the shop doorway? They had no doubt heard Prime Minister David Lloyd George promise the nation that his government was going to ensure that it built a 'land fit for heroes'. Whether or not this couple believed him is another matter.

Right: This brand spanking new bicycle was the first prize in a competition that was advertised as being open to boys and girls only. Although the winner must have been delighted with her success, she must have wondered about the decorum of riding such a bike as it had a crossbar. Whether modesty or bravado won the day, we will never know. The presentation took place in 1935 at 2 Queen Street, Redcar outside the new Dormand Stewart and Sons clothing shop. Particularly noted for its raincoats, the company also had an outlet on Linthorpe Road in Middlesbrough. The family name lives on in Stewart Park, Marton, where the Captain Cook Museum can be found. The grounds that were owned by the Bolckow family interested the local council as a recreational amenity for the town. Because it could not raise sufficient funding, Councillor Thomas Dormand Stewart stepped in with his own personal gift. He paid £28,000 for the estate and gave it to the town as 'a public possession, open and accessible to all the people for all time'. Stewart died in 1946 after being made a Freeman of the Borough in recognition of his service and philanthropy. Today, it is interesting to note the choice of stole that we can see being worn. Real animal fur was all the rage, but just imagine the uproar that there would be now against such a fashion statement.

Right: This junction of Corporation Road and Linthorpe Road, known as Newhouse Corner, has always been a popular spot for shoppers. In c1930, money was tight with so many on the dole. Despite that circumstance, Christmas was coming up and even the poorest of families did its best for the little ones and tried to bring a sparkle to their eyes. J Newhouse's department store occupied the corner site, hence the name of this part of town. Later, it was Binns that became a favourite place to spend what hard earned money there was, or you could just enjoy strolling through the various sections of the shop. George Binns founded a modest drapery business in Sunderland, in 1807, but it is the major stores developed by his grandson, JJ Binns, that we recall. In the early 20th century there were many Binns' outlets across the northeast as the name became synonymous with stylish, but value for money, shopping. The empire was swallowed up by a larger one, the House of Fraser, in the 1950s, but the Binns' name and, therefore its reputation, was retained for many years to come. The children waiting to cross the road would have been looking forward to a visit to Father Christmas in his grotto. A simple gift, such as a penny whistle or a magic colouring book, meant so much to youngsters who had so little back then. As Kitty Kallen would later sing, 'Little things mean a lot'.

Above: This electricity showroom was in Redcar and Snow White and her seven vertically challenged friends were given the task of attracting custom in through the door. The little fellows were used to digging in the mine and the fair lady more accustomed to gazing into a mirror and avoiding tainted apples, but someone had decided that this was the ideal way to promote the sale of electrical appliances. A new Hoover could be tried out before the customer committed to their purchase. The modern upright vacuum cleaner was invented by the American, Murray Spangler, an asthma sufferer whose condition was not helped by beating carpets with sticks or paddles. He was employed by Hoover, then a saddle maker, and the company bought the rights in 1908. The 'beats, as it sweeps as it cleans' formula, which was to become the machine's slogan, was introduced to Hoover machines in 1926. The company was so successful that its name became synonymous with all vacuum cleaners, whatever their make. The jingle used to promote Hoover on early television adverts is now part of our heritage. 'You'll wonder where the yellow went' for Pepsodent toothpaste, 'the too good to hurry mint' for Murraymint and 'Don't be vague, ask for Haig', the whisky distillery, are just some of the other classics from the time when ITV went on air.

Right: Middlesbrough Co-op was part of the movement begun on Toad Lane, Rochdale by the Pioneers who established their society as a mutual trading group that could both benefit themselves and their customers by pooling resources, buying in bulk and passing on the savings. Ordinary shoppers becamc members and shared in the dividend, known to all as 'the divvy', by collecting stamps that were put on a card and exchanged for further goods or discount when the card was filled. From the modest start made in East Lancashire in 1843, the Co-operative Wholesale Society, as it came to be known, expanded its influence across the country until it cornered a large part of the retail and even insurance market either side of the last war. This building, Victoria House, on the corner of Linthorpe Road and Clifton Street, did not make it past 1942. It was gutted by incendiaries on 25th July during one of the air raids. Ironically, the Emporium, as many knew it, had a basement that was used as a shelter and many local residents were taking cover there when the bombs hit. It was furnished with double bunk beds and people took with them small attaché cases filled with some of their most precious possessions, along with flasks of tea and sandwiches. Often they stayed only one or two hours until the all-clear sounded, but on this occasion it was the crash of the bombs exploding that they heard. The Co-op was reduced to a heap of smoking bricks and those in the shelter were lucky to escape with their lives.

Left: It was the swinging 60s and Kings Road was busy with shoppers and a series of vehicles parked up by the kerb. But this was not the street in Chelsea that runs from Sloane Square and across towards Fulham. This was North Ormesby which was not quite the centre of hippie culture, boutiques and chic bars and cafés. Norman's Grill and Snack Bar was not quite ready for kinky boots, long haired men and girls wearing pelmets rather than skirts when this photograph was taken. North Ormesby has seen many changes in more recent years as much of its original housing has been demolished to make way for new developments and the restructuring of the A66 Redcar to Penrith road. With its location close to the Riverside Stadium, the streets are often filled on match days with supporters on their way to watch a soccer game. The land in this neck of the woods once belonged to the Pennyman family of Ormesby Hall, who lived there until the 1980s when the National Trust acquired the estate. Several of the cars we can see show evidence of an American styling, with their tail fins and large chrome bumpers and radiator grilles. They were a far cry from the humble black family saloons that we were used to in the previous decade.

Above: Newhouse's store proclaimed on its awning that this site was 'The Corner' in town and you could not argue with that statement. It was and still is a prominent position on the corner of Linthorpe Road from which to do business. Newhouse's, like so many other independent department stores, was later taken into the Debenham's family of retail outlets. Across the way, Burton, 'the tailor of taste' as it liked to be known, also occupied a prime position from which to dress the male population of the area. Ladies outfitters and men's tailoring was conducted from separate premises until the unisex salons and boutiques made their appearance in the swinging 60s. Before their arrival, a visit to a clothes shop was a formal experience and an established routine, especially in men's tailoring. John Collier, Weaver to Wearer and the Fifty Shilling Tailor all catered for men of all ages who wanted cheap, hardwearing clobber. Made to measure and bespoke outfits were still provided by more specialist firms, but most wanted something 'off the peg'. It mattered little if you were 16 or 60, as a suit was a suit after all. Young men dressed in a similar fashion to their fathers before them and it was only in the 1950s, with the emergence of the teenager as a separate species, that a push for something a little different became noticeable.

TRANSPORT

No view of Middlesbrough would be complete without sight of the internationally famous transporter bridge. This remarkable piece of engineering is the only working example of its type in England. The travelling compartment is suspended by cables from a carriage that runs along the girders, taking two and a half minutes to cross the Tees from Port Clarence. It can take up to nine vehicles at a time and transport several hundred pedestrians 160 feet above the waters of the river below. The bridge even has its place in movie history, being featured in 'Billy Elliott', the story of a young ballet dancer. It also featured in TV's 'Auf Wiedersehen Pet' when it was supposedly dismantled, leaving the BBC to put out a disclaimer as irate viewers thought the storyline was for real. The idea for this novel manner of crossing the Tees was first floated by Charles Smith of Hartlepool Ironworks in the 1870s. His plans were first taken up in Bilbao, Spain, where a transporter was built in 1893. It took a Parliamentary Bill in 1907 to enable Middlesbrough's version to be started. Crossing the Tees was a major problem for the several thousand workers in Port Clarence for most of them lived on the other side of the river. Crossing it twice a day in the ferry boats that were operating was a time consuming and frustrating exercise. The rush to get to the boats at either end of the shifts led to much jostling and many an argument, not to mention the amount of wasted time that was experienced. The vagaries of tides and the weather added to the problems and it was not uncommon for the usual 20 minutes for a crossing to become over an hour, leading to a loss of wages and decreased productivity.

A public meeting was held in Middlesbrough Town Hall in January 1907 and a resolution was made to commission the building of the transporter bridge. Once government permission had been given, a tender from the Glaswegian firm of Sir William Arrol and Company was accepted. The steel truss that spans 565 feet from tower to tower, balanced by the cantilevered end spans of 140 feet each, took some four years to complete. The opening ceremony took place on 7 October 1911 and was conducted by Prince Arthur of Connaught. His standing in the hierarchy reflected the grandeur of the bridge as he was the cousin of King George V and the most senior male member of the Royal Family over the age of 18 to reside in the United Kingdom. As such, he undertook a wide variety of duties on behalf of the monarchy, and acted as a Counsellor of State during periods of the King's absence abroad.

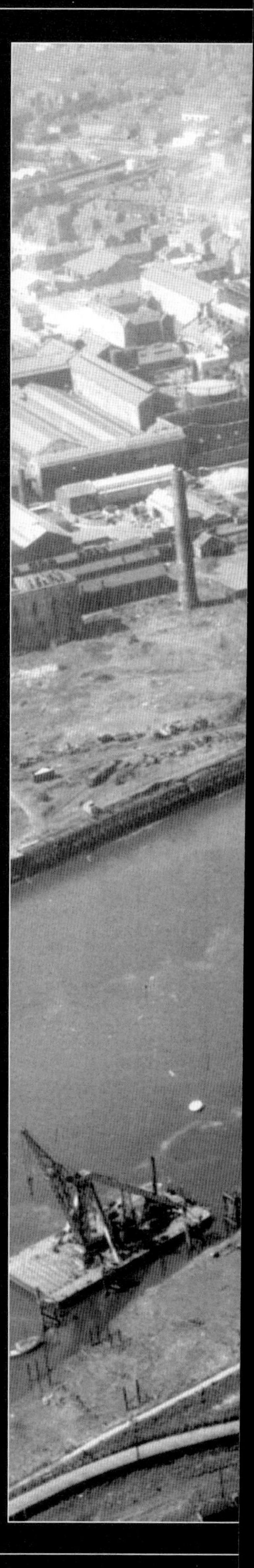

Below: Motoring in the 1920s began to attract private companies who could operate as rivals to the public transport offered by local councils. This charabanc, perhaps the ultimate stretch limousine of its day, operated on the Redcar-Marske-Saltburn route. By the look of the tyres, it must have been a bumpy ride. The open top was an attractive feature, but it must be said that the drawbacks of such a ride in our northern climate are rather obvious. But, in the height of summer, the breeze flowing through your hair must have been quite exhilarating as the vehicle bowled along the road. Heads would turn at such an unusual sight, since most people were still as accustomed to seeing a horse and cart as they were to a motor bus. This form of charabanc was also particularly popular with private parties going off on a day trip. Office workers or neighbours living on a particular street would hire one and set off for a jolly at the seaside or out into the country. Life on the open road was an adventure and was a change from the train journeys that had long become common or garden. The 'chara', as it was usually abbreviated, was something new and everyone was keen to avail himself of getting first hand experience of modern technology.

Above: It could have been a convention for fans of 'The Untouchables', the old television show about American mobsters and ace detective Elliot Ness, but these cars on The Stray at Redcar were lined up as families enjoyed more legal pursuits. No-one was going to jump on a running board and aim a machine gun at anyone today. In the mid 1930s, the sands below the Stray were used by speed merchants. This was nothing to do with the sort of 'speed' that has sadly come to be a part of some youth culture here when night falls today, but the real meaning of the word. Once upon a time, horses raced along the shore. After they moved to the enclosed track in the late 1800s, sand yachts often did battle with one another as they cleverly used the wind to pick up sufficient pace to defeat their rivals. In the interwar years, motor car racing became popular and it was not just the more specialised models that roared across the sands. Ordinary saloons whizzed along as well. Families could enjoy a picnic as they watched the spectacle below. After all, the fun was free and that is always something to be noted. Elsewhere, world land speed records were set on sandy beaches. Pendine, in Wales, was where Malcolm Campbell first drove Bluebird to fame.

Below: These early trams rattled along a tree lined avenue in Norton. Nos 22 and 24 were examples of the first electrically operated public service vehicles in operation. Their open tops provided passengers with a fine view of the surrounding countryside, but were very draughty and uncomfortable in the bad weather that is all too frequent a visitor to Teesside. With the growth in population around Stockton and the rapidly expanding Middlesbrough, there were major calls for a complementary addition to the railways. Both horse and steam power was tried, with mixed success. The real expansion of the services came with the harnessing, not of animals, but of the new wonder of the age – electricity. Several independent companies had operated the first trams, but they were taken under the control of Imperial Tramways in 1896. An electrified tramway was introduced two years later on a three foot seven inch gauge of track. The initial services ran from Norton to North Ormesby and from Stokesley to Middlesbrough. Trams have a special place in our hearts. Who can think of San Francisco without picturing the trolley cars, as Americans refer to them, running on their special cables? Judy Garland even sang about them in the 1944 movie 'Meet me in St Louis'. They have made a comeback in England in such diverse spots as Croydon, Sheffield and Manchester in recent years.

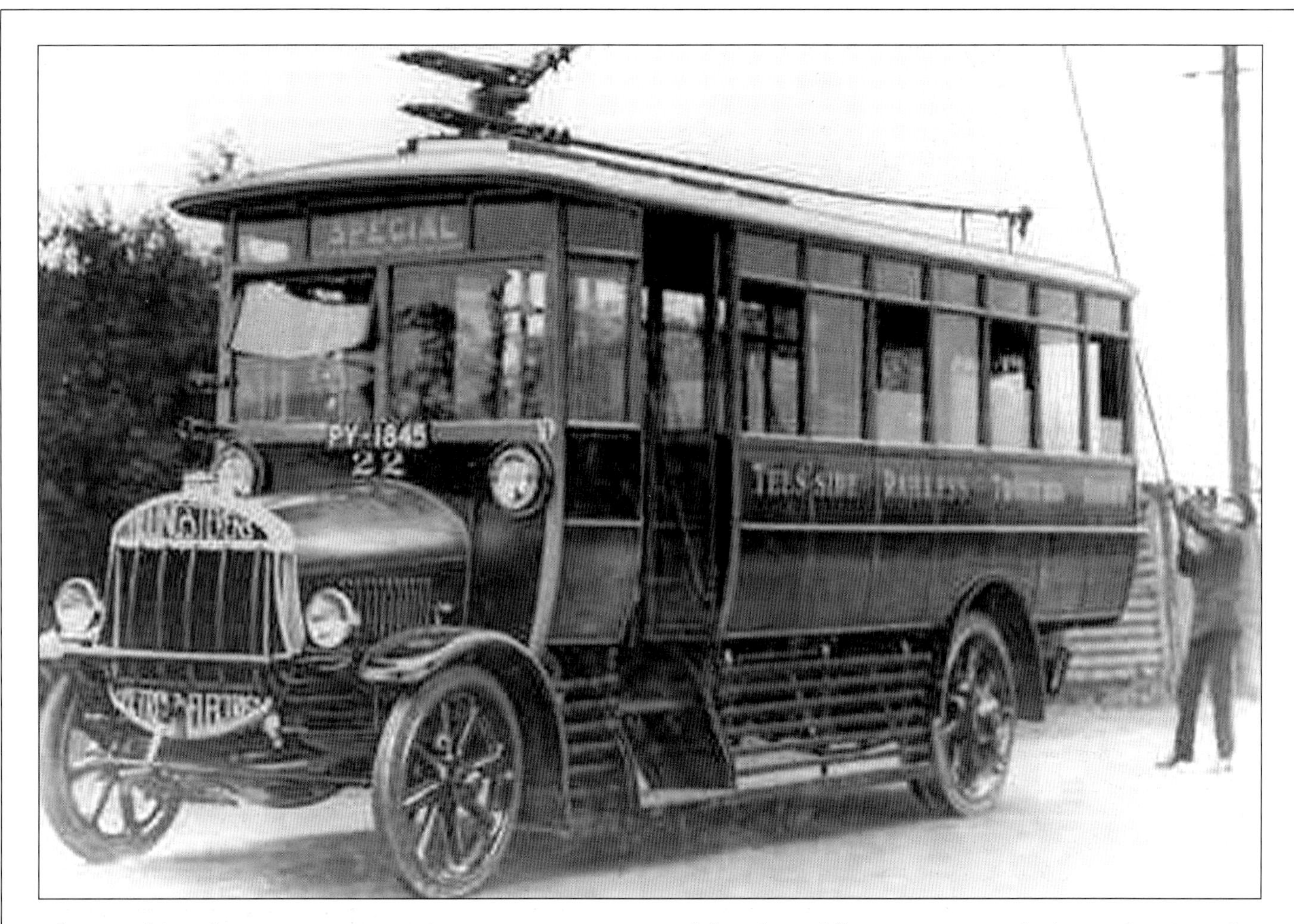

Above: This rather strange contraption was an attempt to marry two sources of power. We still try to do this on our roads today with cars that can switch between petrol and liquid gas as an attempt is made to counter greenhouse emissions. This hybrid in the photograph was a petrol-electric vehicle that operated on the Normanby Road to Eston route from 1924. We can see the driver of the No 22 Special using a pole to help attach the pantograph, the metal frame on top of the bus, to the electric cabling above. The first trolley buses appeared in 1919, built by the Cleveland Car Company of Darlington. They were among the first of their type in the country. This unique vehicle in the photograph was built by Straker-Clough, a name created by two companies that joined forces in 1921. Clough, Smith and Company, a firm of engineers and contractors, was founded in 1910. It commissioned Straker-Squire of Edmonton, London to build the chassis for a series of trolley buses that included this unusual one and marketed it under the Straker-Clough banner. In all, some 63 vehicles of the conventional type were built before the southern company went into liquidation. The hybrid was an almost unique vehicle in the history of British transport with its petrol driven dynamo that drove the traction motor when electric wiring was unavailable.

Right The public transport revolution took Britain by storm in the last few years of Queen Victoria's reign when horse drawn trams were replaced by those that drew their energy sources from the electric cabling that crisscrossed our towns. In this, Stockton was just like everywhere else. But, it had an advantage over many of its contemporaries. High Street was a broad highway that could cope with twin tram tracks. They were laid along the eastern side of the street, leaving plenty of room on the opposite side where carters and stallholders could operate comfortably. In the midst of the crowded scene, we can see the No 7 tram on its way to Thornaby. It is not unreasonable to think that the photograph was taken on Monday 16 July 1898, the day that the service was inaugurated in the town. There appear to be quite a few dignitaries on board and the occasion must have been very special to bring so many out onto the street. The service was operated by Imperial Tramways until 1921 when Middlesbrough, Stockton and Thornaby Corporations each bought an appropriate share of the company. They retained the vermillion and white livery but both town crests were added to the waist panels. The latter pair operated jointly until 1930 when Thornaby passed over its holding to Stockton. Even so, the whole area's transport system would not be properly reunified until Teesside Borough was formed in 1968.

Above: Gaily decorated and painted for its special occasion, the 1932 Daimler single decker No 46 bus was attractively prepared for the coronation celebrations. The coachwork, provided by Middlesbrough firm WG Edmond, was highly polished for its journey and the 32 passengers felt honoured to be on board. On 12 May 1937, George VI received the crown that had been intended for his brother. The schism of the abdication crisis was put to one side and the country rallied behind their new monarch as he made his way into Westminster Abbey. There were parades and processions all across the country as the population partied. Public buildings were festooned with Union flags and banners proclaiming loyalty to the new king and queen. Every town had its own May queen and she rode on a float behind a marching band as part of the festivities. It was quite usual at the time for public transport vehicles to be included in the merriment. They had been decked out in similar fashion two years earlier when George V marked his silver jubilee. Middlesbrough operated single decker buses for many years, only introducing its first twin deck in 1929, when a three axle Guy was purchased. By the end of the 1930s, more and more of the larger buses appeared on the streets. The XG 1389 Daimler was sold off in 1946, by which time there were only a handful of its sort still operating.

AT WORK

Even in 1920, there was still a place for the noble steed as a working animal. Farmers ploughed their fields behind such strong animals, shire horses pulled brewers' drays and forestry workers and lumber merchants called upon their immense power to help them move predigous loads. These logs were awaiting transportation from the station at Hutton Gate, near Guisborough. One of the large estates in the area belonged to the Pease family who were part of the Quaker community. The home at Hutton Hall was funded by the commercial success of the Pease interests in iron ore, coal and the railways. Later, the Hall became a centre for refugees from the Spanish Civil War and was then requisitioned as an army barracks in 1940. It was demolished at the end of the war. Hutton Gate Station, seen behind the wagonload of logs, was opened on 25th February 1854 on the Middlesbrough and Guisborough line. Somewhat remarkably, it was originally the private province of the Peases, such was their level of importance in the area. Perhaps since the line was built principally to service the mines, that should not come as too much of a surprise. The station remained in their hands for half a century until it was purchased by the North Eastern Railway in 1904 and turned over to public use. As with everywhere else in the land, Dr Beeching's reorganisation plans affected Hutton Gate and it closed in 1964. The building remains, but walkers and cyclists now go where steam once flourished.

Above: Simple blast furnaces known as bloomeries were used to smelt iron in medieval times from deposits discovered in veins running through established lead mines. But, the growth of the railways and the demands of the developing shipbuilding industry created an urgent requirement for large quantities of iron and, later, steel to service these greedy behemoths. The first evidence of the iron making on a large scale was seen on Tyneside, but the discovery of large, local deposits in the neighbouring hills gave others the opportunity of competing. The great ironworks at Consett and Middlesbrough soon eclipsed many of their rivals. One of the latter can be seen here. By 1859, there were 30 furnaces along the Tees, 14 of which were in South Bank/Eston Junction. In less than 20 years, the total figure had increased to 94. Situated close to the river, Acklam Ironworks was one of these to have arrived on the scene. It originally had four blast furnaces and several refining fires on its 40 acre site. It was owned by Stevenson, Jaques and Company, which also ran the Boosbeck ironstone mines, near Skelton. By the time that the 1970s dawned, there were just five such blast furnaces left. As the new millennium began, a solitary one at Redcar was all that was left of a famous industry.

Below: With the appearance of a Hornby Doublo engine, this locomotive was dwarfed by the mighty crane that lifted it into the air above the dockside in Middlesbrough. The lovely steam locomotive was one of the countless numbers manufactured by the Robert Stephenson and Hawthorn Company. In 1817, Robert Hawthorn founded a marine engineering and shipyard business in Newcastle, but moved into the railway business in 1831 with his first manufacture of a locomotive. By 1870, the original works was exclusively devoted to this industry, with a new plant taking on the marine business. George and Robert Stephenson are the best known father and son in railway engineering. They jointly formed Robert Stephenson and Company in 1823 at the Forth Street Works, Newcastle, the first of its type in the world, and it was here that the locomotives for the Stockton and Darlington Railway were built. The Forth Street works continued to build locomotives until the middle of the 20th century, as did subsidiary works in Darlington. The original factory building still exists as the Robert Stephenson Centre. The Stephenson and Hawthorn companies merged in 1937 and were taken over by the Vulcan Foundry in 1943, later still being subsumed within English Electric. For nostalgia buffs, the chuff of a steam engine is something special and they would just love it if the Mallard or Coronation Scot raced by just once more.

Left: Middlesbrough, like so many other towns that relied on heavy industry such as iron and steel, shipbuilding and coal exports, has had its face changed dramatically as the final third of the last century unfolded. The smoking chimneys and the Victorian works have largely disappeared, leaving behind photograph albums and memories to make the link with the days when we relied on them for our prosperity. Ayresome Iron Works was just one of many that dominated the skyline all over Teesside. It was founded by Gjers, Mills and Company and eventually developed into a massive complex of buildings that included four massive blast furnaces, its own railway sidings and wharf on the river. John Gjers came over to this country from Sweden to attend the Great Exhibition of 1851. Already a knowledgeable engineer, he took up a position as an assistant blast furnace manager at the Ormesby Ironworks three years later. He soon took on the mantle of full manager, before taking charge of Hopkins and Company's Teesside Ironworks in 1862. His reputation as an engineer grew and he went on to design the works at Linthorpe, before building Ayresome in 1870 for a new company in which he was the senior partner. This ironworks reached its top capacity of production in 1937, but felt the pinch after the war and was eventually closed and demolished in 1966.

Below: In the middle of the 19th century, rich deposits of iron were discovered in the Cleveland Hills, near Eston. John Vaughan, at the time a leading ironmaster in Middlesbrough, made the find. He was already in partnership with the German businessman Henry Bolckow and they had established a small foundry and rolling mill making use of ironstone from Durham and Yorkshire. However, the raw material on their own doorsteps presented them with the opportunity to extract ore locally and much more cheaply than before. They built Teesside's first blast furnace in 1851. As the railway age boomed, the need for greater amounts of iron soared, as did the duo's standing and finances. Further furnaces were built and Bolckow used his fame and fortune to move into politics, becoming both the town's first Mayor and first Member of Parliament. As the demand for steel grew, Vaughan and Bolckow turned their attention to the Bessemer process of production, using the methods pioneered in Sheffield. Their stock boomed, as did the town in the second half of the Victorian age. The Newport Iron Works in the photograph was just one of many of its type that provided Teesside with a mixture of prosperity and pollution. The firm of Bolckow and Vaughan was taken over in the late 1920s by Dorman Long, the company that built Sydney Harbour Bridge.

Right: We all know the name of Charlie Chaplin, one of the major figures of 20th century entertainment. Thanks to the likes of presenter and comedian Paul Merton, his silent film exploits, along with those of his contemporaries, are still revived on television on occasions in this century. Although he made his fame and fortune in Hollywood with such 1920s' silent movies as 'The Kid' and 'The Gold Rush', with the later talkie, 'The Great Dictator', he was a star long before he went to America. Born in London in 1889, he was on stage in the music halls as a child star and by the time he was a teenager had earned a reputation as a comic and clown of some repute. In 1906, he joined Casey's Court Circus, a troupe of variety artistes. On 21st February 1906, he played Middlesbrough Empire, a music hall theatre that opened in 1897. Restored to its former glory in 1991, the Empire has played host to many famous names since Chaplin's day, including Morecambe and Wise and the modern day pop groups such as the Scissor Sisters. Chaplin first toured America with Fred Karno's chaotic, slapstick 'army' in 1910, before making his home over there when he moved into films in 1914, though he always retained his British citizenship. Chaplin was a versatile man. He even composed a number one hit with 'This is my song', recorded by Petula Clark in 1967.

Bottom right: If you thought that women on Blue Watch was a relatively modern phenomenon, think again. Firefighters, as we now must call them, contained members of the so called weaker sex many, many years ago. It is perhaps a poignant thought that it took two world wars to advance the cause of women's equality, but their contributions on the factory floor, in the fields, behind the wheel and in uniform were major factors in keeping the country running and winning the conflicts. The blitz on our towns and cities that began in 1940 demonstrated that the organisation of our fire services was ill prepared for the volume of work that came their way during those terrible times. They were still under the control of a variety of local authorities and in 1941, somewhat belatedly, the National Fire Service (NFS) was formed. This helped co-ordinate action more proficiently. With a shortage of personnel, because so many had been called up into the armed forces, women were actively recruited to join the NFS. It continued to exist as a Home Office run service until 1947, the time when this photograph of firewomen was taken during the spring of that year. At least one local young woman was among the first year delegates attending a general course at the No 2 Area residential training school in County Durham.

Above: Soldiers billeted at Redcar in World War II were stationed on the racecourse as they underwent training and exercises that prepared them for the battlefront overseas. Most had no idea where they would end up and the conversation often turned to conjecture about postings to the European theatre, North Africa or the Far East. In the meantime, there was work to be done on the drill ground and the men woke early in the morning and got ready for whatever the day ahead might hold. It was no cushy number. Facilities were spartan as this was no holiday camp. Necessary ablutions often took place in the open air without the privilege of hot water. This picture might look amusing, but the chap receiving the dousing would have had goose pimples all over him. His colleague waiting his turn would have done so with some apprehension. However, the basic conditions were good preparation for a tour of duty at the front as home comforts there would be few and far between. The men who were thrown together built up a level of camaraderie that could never be matched on civvy street. It was essential that they formed bonds with their fellows as they might have to rely upon their help in the most dangerous of circumstances in a few weeks' time.

Right: The famous Transporter Bridge dominates this picture which dates from 1936 - the month is believed to be May. The clarity of the scene belies the fact that the print is over 60 years old. At the time this picture was taken the bridge had been open for only a quarter of a century, having been designed by the Cleveland Bridge and Engineering Company Ltd., with foundation stones being laid on each bank of the river on August 3rd 1910. It remains the largest bridge of its type in the world thanks to its 570ft span across the water and overall width of 850 ft. The bridge cost just over £87,000 to construct and the work was completed in little over a year.

Relph Funeral Services - Serving to the End

Joseph Relph, the great-grandfather of its current manager, Michael Relph, established Middlesbrough's oldest funeral firm, Relph Funeral Service, in 1870.

The very first premises were in Boundary Road, where Joseph, a carpenter by trade, made all the coffins, and from where he also had to be available literally 24 hours a day.

In those days most people did not have easy access to a telephone or transport. People were reliant on an undertaker being local to the point of being virtually on the doorstep: understandably there were far more undertakers than there are today.

Today Relph Funeral Service provides services for bereaved families throughout the Tees Valley and as far away as Scarborough. The current premises at 43 Kings Road, North Ormesby have been occupied since the 1960s.

Modern luxurious limousine transport is very different from the horse-drawn carriages used in the days of Joseph Relph when a man was employed to walk or 'page' in front of the horse: he had a permanent sheen on the back of his black coat from stopping and having the horse walk into his back. Today the traditional horse-drawn hearse is still popular and requested by families on a regular basis.

Over the years the firm has been entrusted with the funeral arrangements for many prominent people, not least, Sir Joseph William Isherwood, Lord Grathorne and Dr Lacey the Catholic Bishop of Middlesbrough: in fact the firm has buried no fewer than four Roman Catholic Bishops.

Considerably more cremations than burials now take place. Because of strict regulations about cremations the materials coffins can be made of have changed greatly. Another change is that unlike the old 'penny policies' that people would rely on to cover the cost of funerals many now opt for pre-planning and pre-paying for their funeral through their funeral director.

Relph Funeral Service is now part of Dignity Plc., a British company. The firm is a member of the National Association of Funeral Directors and the British Institute of Embalmers. Today under Michael Relph the firm still provides exactly what it has been doing since 1870 – as caring and as personal a service as possible.

Top left: *An early twentieth century Relph horsedrawn carriage.* ***Left:*** *Michael Relph, current Manager.* ***Below:*** *Relph Funeral Director & Monumental Consultants, 43 Kings Road, North Ormesby.*

Ridsdale & Co Ltd and Bureau of Analysed Samples Ltd Associates in Control

The phenomenal growth of Middlesbrough throughout the nineteenth century was very largely due to the enormous development within the steel industry during that period.

Following the pioneering work of Henry Bessemer, who patented the first bulk steel making process in 1856, steel production expanded tremendously in the North East of England, and particularly in and around Middlesbrough where substantial deposits of the raw material, iron ore, were found.

At one such operation, namely the North Eastern Steel Works, Mr Charles Ridsdale worked as Chief Chemist and Technical Advisor and was responsible for analysing the chemical composition of the steel grades produced. Recognising the critical importance of accurate analysis of steels, Charles Ridsdale and his son Noel formed Ridsdale & Co as consulting analysts in 1912 and introduced the 'Analoid' system of analysis, for which tabletted reagents are used to determine the elements present in irons and steels by classical chemical analysis.

Around this time two important events occurred in the steel industry. On the positive side, in 1913 Harry Brearley invented stainless steel, which, by introducing other elements such as chromium and nickel at a specified level, greatly expanded the range of products which could be made with steel. On the negative side, the sinking of RMS Titanic in 1912 demonstrated that poor quality could lead to catastrophic failure of steel in hostile conditions. Both these events underlined the need for accurate analysis to ensure that any steel produced was fit for purpose.

The concept of using Standard Samples (or Certified Reference Materials as they are now known) had just been introduced by the then US National Bureau of Standards (NBS), and Charles Ridsdale was quick to see the advantages of such 'benchmarking' materials. The samples were mainly for use within the USA, but the NBS proved to be more than willing to assist Ridsdale & Co to produce its own for the UK market.

As the recognition of the importance of such Standard Samples grew it was decided to set up an informal association of UK Co-operating Analysts under the title of the 'British Chemical Standards Movement (BCS)'. The first BCS samples were issued in 1917, produced through the process of 'round robin' analysis by a group of co-operating laboratories. These soon gained recognition throughout the UK, such that the Iron and Steel Institute (ISI) decided to form a Technical Sub-Committee to prepare Standard Samples on a national basis. The possibility of merging the BCS movement with the ISI

Technical Committee was carefully considered but found to be impracticable. The two organisations thus produced Standard Samples in parallel for a dozen or so years before the ISI Technical Sub-Committee was eventually disbanded after producing only a minimal number of samples.

Following the death of Charles Ridsdale in 1934 it was decided to form a private limited company to ensure that the work of the BCS Movement would continue independently of any one individual. As a result Bureau of Analysed Samples Ltd (BAS) was incorporated in 1935 to take charge of the production and supply of Standard Samples for the UK iron and steel industry. Ridsdale & Co was incorporated as a private limited company at the same time and, in addition to continuing its Consultant Analysis role and production of 'Analoid' tablets, it became licensees to the H W Dietert Co, USA for the manufacture of foundry laboratory sand testing and control equipment.
At the start of its existence, Ridsdale & Co. was established at 1/3 Wilson Street in the centre of Middlesbrough with just half a dozen employees, but by the time BAS was formed the numbers had swelled to 20 and the companies had taken on additional premises at 234 Marton Road. During the second world war the companies were obliged to move out of Middlesbrough and set up temporarily in Markington, near Harrogate, but after that they looked around for larger premises and, importantly, ones which had a clean air environment which was essential to the production of highly accurately analysed Standard Samples. In 1952 they purchased Newham Hall, near Newby, which had been the former home to an Iron Master, Jack Mills, in the late nineteenth century but which had been unoccupied during the war and used only for storage by the MOD.

Noel Ridsdale's son, Peter, had joined the Companies at this time, following service in the armed forces during the war and for two years afterwards. They set about converting the stately home into a laboratory and offices, including establishing a small engineering workshop in the former coach house.

Newham Hall had been relocated from its original site off Ladgate Lane, and the present building, together with its lodge and entrance constructed in 1880, are Grade II listed buildings. Great care has been taken to retain as many features of the buildings in their original form as possible, whilst making the premises a suitable environment for the necessary company activities.

During their tenure at Newham Hall, R&Co and BAS have undergone changes in line with developments in the analytical industry. As laboratories progress from classical chemical methods to instrumental techniques the demand for 'Analoid' tabletted reagents has decreased (though there is a steady demand for indicator tablets) and, latterly, the UK foundry industry has been in decline. This has reduced the demand in

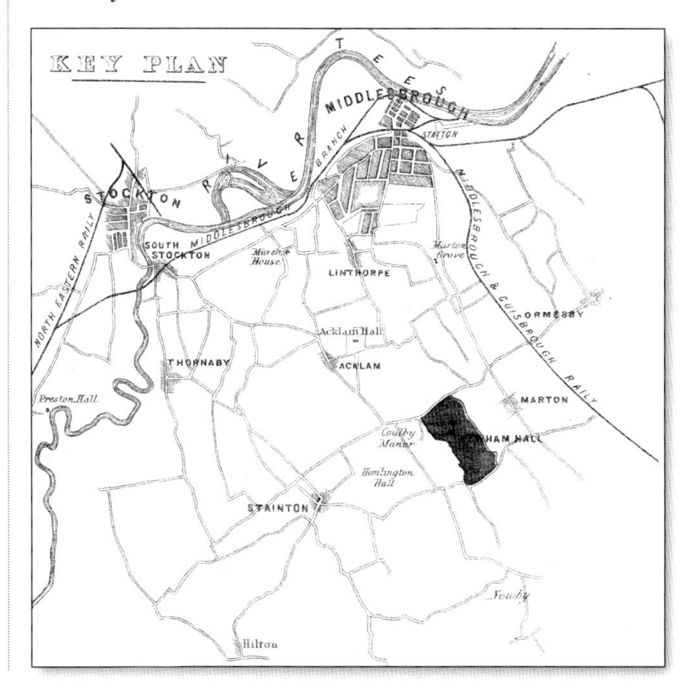

***Top left:** Mr Charles Ridsdale. **Left:** Mr Noel Ridsdale. **Above:** Third generation Mr Peter Ridsdale. **Right:** A plan of the Newham Hall estate from 1874.*

UK for foundry laboratory sand testing and control equipment, and for the associated calibration service which Ridsdale & Co. provides. To counter this a good export trade has been established.

On the other hand, the market for CRMs has grown steadily with the increase in demand for calibration samples for analytical instruments. The advent of Quality Assurance protocols which require the use of authorised CRMs to control analytical methods and procedures has also contributed to growth.

In order to ensure the accuracy, reliability and authenticity of their CRMs, which are critical in providing the means to control the chemical compositions of iron, steel and associated materials, BAS has utilised since 1950 the services of an Honorary Advisory Committee (HAC) consisting of eight to ten Senior Technical Staff from industrial and research organisations, which provides advice on the selection of materials for CRMs, recommendations regarding laboratories to participate in the 'round-robin' analyses, evaluation of results received and most importantly the approval of CRM certificates.

For over 30 years until his death in 1997, Ben Bagshawe, former Chief Chemist of Firth Brown Ltd, Sheffield, was Chairman of the HAC. Ben was awarded an MBE in 1996 for his services to analytical chemistry.

It is through the existence of such an independent and unbiased expert Committee that BAS, as only a small private company of approximately 30 personnel, can rub shoulders with Government-sponsored CRM organisations in other countries.

When the UK joined the European Common Market in 1973, BAS was asked to represent the UK in co-operation with the German Federal Testing Institute (BAM) and the French Iron and Steel Research Institute (IRSID) in the preparation of European (now EURONORM) Certified Reference Materials, under the auspices of the European Coal & Steel Community. This European Group has now been swelled by the addition of the Nordic CRM Working Group, and it oversees all stages of the preparation and certification of EURONORM samples in the same way that the HAC oversees all BAS samples.

Customers of R&Co include most of the foundries in UK, plus many from other countries all over the world. Major customers of BAS include primarily iron and steel producing organisations, the most local of which is Corus (now taken over by Tata Ltd, India), which uses BAS CRMs in all its UK laboratories. However, as these CRMs are eminently exportable, comprising either finely divided material (powder, chippings, or turnings) or discs/blocks, BAS samples are regularly used by companies in over 60 countries worldwide, including steel producers Arcelor, Mittal Steel, POSCO, China Steel Corporation, Sandvik, Voestalpine, non-ferrous and mineral producers such as Alcan, INCO, Lafarge, Pilkington, St. Gobain, and contract laboratories such as the local Bodycote Materials Testing Teesside and the long-established Pattinson & Stead.

Facing page: *Exterior and interior views of Newham Hall.* **Above:** *Mr Ben Bagshawe receives his MBE in 1996.* **Right:** *Dr John Stead.*

One of the co-founders of Pattinson & Stead, formed in 1876 in Zetland Road, but now established in Marton, was the notable Analytical and Consulting Chemist, Dr John Edward Stead who was recorded as the official Borough Analyst in the 1890s. Coincidentally, Charles Ridsdale began his analytical career with Dr Stead, thus forging an early link between the two parties.

Not only have Pattinson & Stead (P&S) been regular customers for BAS CRMs, but they have also been one of the laboratories which participate in the 'round-robin' analyses to certify such samples. When the former Directors of P&S decided to retire in 2005, R&Co/BAS purchased their assets and goodwill to form a third company within the Group. P&S is to be moved to Newham Hall in the near future to consolidate the activities of all the companies on one site.

Sadly, in June 2006, Peter Ridsdale died, having been at the helm for nearly 60 years. He had overseen the strengthening of the Companies within the international community through the approval and recognition of the R&Co/BAS quality System to ISO 9001 in 1994, the accreditation of R&Co laboratory testing facilities to ISO 17025 in 2004, and more recently the accreditation of BAS as a Reference Material Producer to ISO Guide 34 in 2006. Indeed, BAS was extremely proud to be amongst the first group of five UK RM Producers to be accredited to ISO Guide 34. Although, by tragic coincidence, the formalisation of this latter achievement came just two weeks after Peter Ridsdale's death he left behind a strong organisation which is now run by his son-in-law Richard Meeres, a Chemistry Graduate from Oxford University who joined

BAS in 1976 after several years experience with Shell Chemicals and who became Managing Director in 1992.

The aim of the Companies is to continue to adapt to the changing needs of the analytical industry, whilst striving to maintain the sound structure which has been established through three generations of the Ridsdale family. To this end Colin Flintoft, who has been a Director of BAS since 1993 was appointed a Director of R&Co. in 2007. Jane Meeres, a Director of R&Co. since 1989 was appointed Director of BAS in 2007, together with Dr Malcolm Taylor who, as former Chief Chemist of Allvac Ltd (formerly Special Melted Products Ltd, formerly Firth Brown Ltd) has taken over the Chairmanship of the HAC.

Through these appointments, and the continued efforts and diligence of the staff, Ridsdale & Co Ltd, Bureau of Analysed Samples Ltd and Pattinson & Stead (2005) Ltd intend to play their part in the wellbeing of the Middlesbrough area for many years to come.

Above: *Directors Mr Richard Meeres, Mr Peter Ridsdale and Mr Colin Flintoft pictured in 2006.* ***Below:*** *A staff group photograph receiving an Award for export achievement in 1997.*

Lithgow Sons & Partners

Lithgow Sons & Partners, today based at the Auction Houses, Station Rd, Stokesley, traces its roots back to 1868 when Samuel Lithgow commenced business as an auctioneer, valuer and furniture dealer in the Market Place in Middlesbrough.

In 1879 Samuel entered into partnership with John Robert Storry. Though that partnership would be amicably dissolved in 1904 the Storry story was in fact far from over: in 1954 David H Storry would join S Lithgow and Sons Ltd and take the company forward into the 21st century.

Meanwhile the Lithgow business moved to Albert Road in 1896.

Samuel Lithgow's son James ran the business until his own death in 1934. His son, James Lithgow junior, now carried on the business on his own for a number of years.

In 1970 David Storry purchased the first half of the current Stokesley site and a move was made to there in 1971. That same year James Lithgow, who had been involved in the business since 1934 retired. Jo Smith another stalwart retired in 1981 and Bill Carter three years later.

Meanwhile David Storry had acquired the other half of the site in 1979. The Albert Road offices in Middlesbrough closed in 1985.

Today the company specialises in arranging and conducting auctions of all forms of industrial and commercial goods and properties, either on-site or from its Auction Houses in Stokesley. In addition the company provides Asset Valuation and Disposal, Commercial Property Valuations, Residential Property and Storage Services.

The firm also acts as a Commercial Property agency for properties throughout the region including shops, offices, licensed premises and industrial properties.

Auction facilities at Station Road, Stokesley include nine salerooms totalling 33,000 sq. ft., lifting facilities up to five tons, two acres of tarmac car parking, loading ramp, and computerised accounting.

Monthly sales are held of Tools and Equipment; Household Furniture and Antique Furniture; Plant and Equipment; Motor Cars and Commercial Vehicles; Catering Equipment; Office Furniture and IT Equipment; Shop and Liquidated Stock. Six-monthly sales are held of Fine Wines and Boats.

The next generation - Richard Storry - joined the business in 1989. David Storry retired in 2000.

Left: *Lithgow Sons & Partners old Albert Road premises.* ***Above:*** *Auction Houses, Station Road, Stokesley, home to Lithgow Sons & Partners, 2007.*

Huntsman Pigments Division

Today Huntsman is a leading global producer of titanium dioxide pigments. Its TIOXIDE® brand name is recognized all over the world. The business employs approximately 2,000 people worldwide, and has factories in seven countries with a combined total capacity of some 550,000 tonnes a year.

From its headquarters site in Haverton Hill Road in Billingham what is now the Huntsman Pigments Division has been a major presence in the area since 1934.

Titanium dioxide pigments provide whiteness and opacity to a vast range of everyday products from coatings and plastics, to inks and even cosmetics and food.

To produce the pigment the company processes a raw material rich in titanium from minerals found in beach sands and rock. This feedstock is treated to extract the titanium and then reforms it as titanium dioxide to a very closely defined particle size. Finally the product is coated and milled to produce a range of versatile pigments for key end uses.

The seven acre plot of land in Billingham was bought in 1933 for just £1,000 by what was then British Titan Products, a business whose roots already stretched back many decades, and on an international stage with early enterprises in Britain, the USA and Scandinavia.

It was on 10th July 1933 that the first earth was turned in the green field site just off Haverton Hill Road. The new titanium dioxide factory would cost £142,899 to build. Though unemployment was rife in a world fallen into a catastrophic economic recession, by May the next year the factory was complete and in production, offering jobs for work starved Teessiders.

Above left: *Reverend William Gregor.* ***Below:*** *The foundations of the first Billingham chimney, August 1933. Built by H Forde Clarke the chimney was 200 feet high with a diameter of 19 feet 5 inches. Pictured from left to right are Patricia Stopford (sitting on the wall) C J Stopford, Works Manager, Mrs Moelbach and Mrs Stopford.* ***Right:*** *The first factory model for Billingham Works, inset, and the completed factory in the late 1930s.*

The story however can be traced back much further, to one day in 1790 when the Reverend William Gregor, then living in Diptford in Cornwall and a keen amateur mineralogist, received a small parcel of black sand that had been found in the Menaccan Valley in Cornwall.

Gregor ascertained that the 'sand', which was given the name Menaccanite, was a compound of iron with traces of manganese, but it also contained another previously unknown substance. He found that a magnet attracted the black grains away from the ordinary silica sand. These he treated with hydrochloric acid and dissolved out iron oxide leaving a white residue which with some difficulty he dissolved in sulphuric acid. From this solution, by treatment with soda and after calcinations, he obtained a white powder. This was the very first time titanium dioxide had been produced. Five years later an Austrian chemist, Martin Klaproth, analysing a similar ore named the previously unnamed metallic element Titanium.

When vast deposits of Menaccanite were later found in the Ilmen mountains in Russia the mineral would be renamed Ilmenite.

The industrial production of titanium dioxide began in the USA in 1906 by TAM the Titanium Alloy Manufacturing Company at a factory near Niagara Falls. In 1916 TPC also based at Niagara Falls went into production.

Meanwhile large deposits of ilmenite had been found in Egersund in Norway. In 1912 a research centre as established near Oslo. The result of that venture was the establishment in 1916 of the first European company for the production of titanium dioxide, the Titan Company. It began large-scale production from a new factory at Fredrikstad at the end of the first world war.

TPC and Titan would soon cooperate with one another to share patents.

Meanwhile RW Greef & Co Ltd was the sole concessionaire in the UK for the Norwegian company, Titan. Greef promoted titanium dioxide heavily at various exhibitions, trade fairs and in magazines. Greef's Noel Heaton BSc FCS in particular was very active in marketing and sales. In the 1920s RW Greef & Co had a Titanium White stand at the Building Exhibition at Olympia.

White lead had been a common constituent of paint products. Lead being poisonous, many fatalities had ensued. By contrast 'titanium white' appeared to be a remarkably benign product. This characteristic was dramatically demonstrated at Olympia in 1924 where according to the Journal of Decorative Art for May of that year, " Messrs Greef have always displayed great ingenuity in their methods of demonstrating the now well established qualities of titanium white, but at their stand at Olympia they showed some which surpasses their previous best"

"Among the virtues of titanium white is its non-poisonous quality. Challenged on this point Mr Noel Heaton consumed 1lb of the pigment. X-ray photographs were taken at intervals and these exhibited at the stand, showed the pigment passing through the body. The last traces were not eliminated for two days, so that the pigment had every chance of disclosing any poisonous quality. Mr Heaton felt no ill effects, and so had a conclusive answer to any person bold enough to suggest that the titanium is otherwise than harmless. He must surely become famous as the most thorough going of believers in any paint material.

Heaton was apparently starved for 16 hours before his titanium meal which consisted of about a pound of titanium white extra X dust grade, made up into a cream with water containing a little glucose and gum Arabic. This experiment, complete with X-rays, is not one likely to be repeated in modern times!

In 1927 the titanium dioxide industry began in Britain with the formation of National Titanium Pigments Ltd (NTP) later called Laporte. This company initially operated using a pilot plant in Barking, which continued for five years before it built a larger plant in Luton.

It was in 1930 that a second British company made its appearance on the scene: the British Titan Products Company Ltd (BTP). This would be the forerunner of Huntsman's Pigments business.

British Titan Products had been formed originally as a subsidiary of the Imperial Smelting Corporation which was a manufacturer of white lead, a substance now under threat by the new product. By 1933 its shares were owned by a group of four different companies all with an interest in the field.

Billingham in the north of England was good selection for a new factory site because ilmenite was available using the short sea crossing across the North Sea from Norway and could be unloaded at the deep sea port on the River Tees. There was a good source of water, by-product coke oven gas, and cheap piped sulphuric acid from nearby ICI (itself a 20 per cent shareholder in the new company). Large quantities of raw materials for 'extenders' could be mined nearby, and the actual site was deep hard clay which was ideal for building.

The original design in Billingham had been for an annual output of 1,600 tons of white TiO2 pigment, but even as the factory opened this target was being increased to 3,000 tons. By 1937 plans were afoot to raise production to 7,000 tons a year.

During the second world war the factory suffered from shortages of raw materials, but nevertheless made a major contribution to the war effort, not least filling shells with titanium tetrachloride used by the armed forces to make smoke.

In the war years the threat of enemy bombing was ever present. Firewatchers kept a look out from what was known as the crows nest. A note signed by the works manager CJ Stopford written on 30th October 1940 expresses his concern for the firewatchers well being:

"I realise that a long spell in the crows nest will be very uncomfortable but even so it is essential that one always keeps a look out i.e. that only one sit down at a time. To help conditions in a very long alarm period, as from today a tin of biscuits and some oxo cubes will be left in this room each evening. They, together with an electric kettle, should be taken up to the crows nest the first time you go on duty and left up there the rest of the night. They will be brought down and replenished by day staff each day and left here for the next night."

Air raids were numerous, and though the factory was never hit, there was one unforgettable night when the petrol tanks opposite the plant received a direct hit. The entrance gate and all of that area became a mass of men, hoses and fire appliances: the telephone switchboard became the nerve centre of the fire fighting operations.

Potential bombing of the site was only one problem which had to be met. Supplies of raw materials were being sunk at sea by enemy action. The German invasion of Norway was the greatest blow, leading to the loss of supplies of that vital ore: Norwegian ilmenite. New sources had to be found quickly, and a variety of ores from all over the world made an appearance in Billingham. Ore from Malaya, India, Portuguese East Africa, Tasmania and

Far left, facing page: *C J Stopford, General Manager and W S Robinson, Chairman of BTP, present Sir Robert Horne MP with the honour of pulling the lever to fill the first barrel of Kronos titanium dioxide, July 1934.* ***Above:*** *Billingham Laboratory, 1934.* ***Above left:*** *Chlorine tankers in Billingham Works. 60% came by road and 40% by rail. However after 1965 the tanker movements ceased as chlorine came by pipeline from ICI.*

many other places strained the ingenuity of staff. The plant capacity was severely affected by using these different ores. For example using Indian ilmenite the plant capacity was 13 to 14 tons per day compared to 20 tons per day using Norwegian ilmenite.

Nor was the supply of ores the only problem. Scrap iron used in processing was also needed for the manufacture of armaments, whilst sulphuric acid, another important ingredient, was rationed. In addition people from every part of the workforce were called up to join the armed forces, leaving those remaining to tackle extra duties.

Post-war, the year 1949 saw the opening of the Billingham research and development laboratories which were well equipped to aid production and give the best possible technical service to customers. At the end of 1948 sanction was given for further new research laboratories to be built when the opportunity arose.

In December 1955 Billingham Works set up a record when it competed 127 consecutive days, representing 400,000 working hours, without a lost time incident. The board marked the occasion by awarding a ten-shilling safety bonus per man.

In those years production was stepped up once more. There was a period of relative stability during the second half of the 1950s and the early 1960s when production reached 20,000 tons.

Further expansion came in 1963 when it was decided to expand production from 21,000 to 27,000 tpa. £1,172,000 was invested.

Billingham produced pigment solidly for the next ten years until an expansion proposal was put up to increase production by another 5,000 tons. This level of production had been discussed as early as 1943. It would however create a major problem in disposing of all the waste acid and ferrous sulphate effluent. However an effluent discharge licence was due to expire in 1976 and to renew it would necessitate the expenditure of more than half a million pounds. Despite some discussion about the future of the plant approval for the expenditure was provisionally given the go ahead.

Celebrations were premature. Environmental pressures with the need to clean up the Tees as well as fixed costs made closure economically inevitable. The final decision was taken in July 1980 for closure of the plant by June 1981. The Billingham site was cleared except for offices and some other buildings which could be used for other purposes. Production was transferred to other plants.

Happily however the Billingham story was far from over. After lying all but deserted for several years the site began to return to life again as some of the old buildings were restructured for modern usage, being turned into laboratories and semi-technical experimental work. With cost saving measures in the 1990s developments accelerated and additional buildings were erected to accommodate the transfer of staff from the Group's other laboratories when they closed.

Slowly but surely the whole of the Group's technical division became centralised on the site.

Meanwhile changes in ownership were afoot. BTP had become BTP Tioxide in 1975, and in 1982 become Tioxide UK Ltd followed by Tioxide Europe Ltd. In 1999 Tioxide was taken over by Huntsman and renamed Huntsman Tioxide. By 2000 the old works site at Billingham had a new future as the consolidated headquarters of the Huntsman Tioxide Group. Today the Billingham site is a vital part of the Huntsman Pigments Division.

An international business, based in the USA, Huntsman itself is a global manufacturer and marketer of differentiated chemicals. Its operating companies manufacture products for a variety of global industries, including chemicals, plastics, automotive, aviation, textiles, footwear, paints and coatings, construction, technology, agriculture, health care, detergent, personal care, furniture, appliances and packaging.

Originally known for pioneering innovations in packaging and, later, for rapid and integrated growth in petrochemicals, Huntsman today has 13,000 employees and operates from multiple locations worldwide. In 2006 the company had worldwide sales of over $13 billion.

The Huntsman Pigments Division story was compiled from the publication 'From British Titan Products to Huntsman Tioxide, A Company History 1930 to 2000', by J.M.Graham, 2001.

***Top left,** facing page: Billingham Wet Treatment expansion in 1964. **Below:** Billingham site pictured in July 2000.*

Middlesbrough College - Education for All

Middlesbrough College is the largest provider of post sixteen education and training within the Tees Valley: it employs some 500 teaching staff and caters for many thousands of learners. The college offers a full range of academic, vocational and professional programmes, including tailor-made provision for local and national businesses.

In various guises the College has been providing education and training relevant to the needs of local people for many decades.

In September 2008 the College will move into brand new premises at the heart of Middlesbrough as part of the Middlehaven regeneration scheme. In doing so it will vacate four sites which have been important parts of the educational fabric of Middlesbrough for nearly a century, including one site which contains the only Grade One listed building in the area.

That listed building is Acklam Hall, originally built in the 17th century as a private residence.

In the reign of Edward the Confessor the manor of Acklam, tended mainly by descendents of former Danish invaders was of great worth. After the Conquest of 1066 the Normans laid waste the land, despoiled the English and inflicted new overlords upon them. The Boynton family, in the shape of Sir Ingram Boynton of Acklam, first appears in the 13th century.

In 1612 Sir Francis Boynton rented Acklam Grange to William Hustler a wealthy draper from Bridlington, and in 1637 Francis' son Matthew Boynton sold Acklam Grange to William Hustler. The Hustler family's association with Acklam Hall would last over 300 years.

William Hustler's grandson, also called William, was knighted in 1678, and in 1683 he built Acklam Hall – the date featured on the ornate ceiling at the head of the staircase. It was built in the fashion of the time showing some Dutch influence in the

***Top:** Acklam Hall, 1936. **Right:** The Assembly Hall in 1936.*

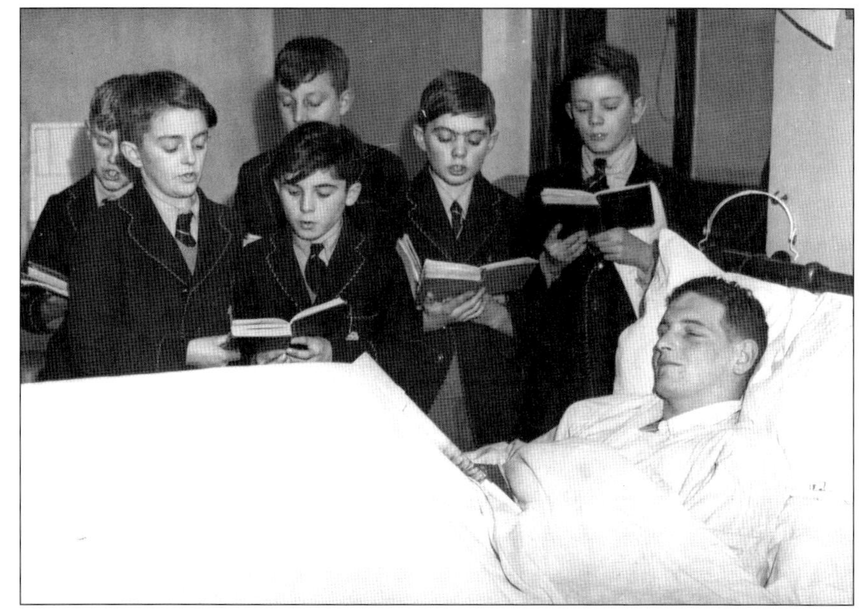

£22,000 was spent on clearing outbuildings, adapting, extending and furnishing and equipping the property to enable it to open as a school.

Acklam Hall Secondary School opened in 1935 with 231 pupils. The first headmaster was Mr R Gill, who was succeeded by Mr J Hurst from 1947 and Mr W Rowlands in 1966. The official opening ceremony for the new school took place on 23rd July 1936. The ceremony was performed by Councillor J Wesley Brown, after which there was a display of physical training followed by tea on the lawn.

Between 1951 and 1958 the remaining ornamental gardens were removed and extensions built for Acklam Hall Grammar School, at a cost of £82,046.

The extensions comprised a two storey teaching block with attached single storey practical rooms, linked to the old building to the east by a new assembly hall with stage and entrance vestibule. The new wing had on the ground floor two classrooms, two art and crafts rooms, and two woodwork rooms, and on the first floor five classrooms access to which was provided by two staircases. A corridor running behind the stage gave access to the ground floor teaching rooms which were readily available for use as 'green rooms'. The assembly hall with a floor area of 3,150 sq ft had a fully-equipped stage with storage below, and opened onto a new vestibule entrance which would now constitute the main entrance to the school

gables. The main approach the Hall was by way of a splendid avenue of lime and fir trees extending for nearly half a mile. Many of those trees would survive until the great storm of 7th January 1829. Several alterations were made to the building down the years, not least those made in 1912 by Mr Walter Brierley when the attic, originally built in the Gothic style of the mid 19th century, was re-built and a new dining room and kitchens added.

In 1928 the Hall and grounds of 56 acres, including the tree-lined avenue and land almost to Ladgate Lane, were bought by Middlesbrough Corporation from Mostyn Hustler. The auctioneer's list suggests that no other bids were received: the sum offered by the Corporation was £11,500. A further

Top left: *Pupils sing carols to a convalescing soldier in 1944.* ***Above left:*** *Junior and Senior winners of the Chess Association are congratulated, 1952.* ***Below:*** *Students gather to watch an experiment in the Chemistry Laboratory in 1954.*

through which access could be gained to the old building. At the time it was wryly noted that that 'attic bedrooms can have their disadvantages when used as classrooms.'

These new extensions enabled the school to accommodate 540 pupils including 90 in the sixth form.

In 1967 Acklam Hall Grammar School for Boys became the 13-18 non-selective Acklam High School. It also became co-educational by amalgamating with Kirby Girls Grammar School, which was then closed. By 1971 the last flower beds had been removed to pave the way for a separate sixth form building, accommodating 540 pupils. In addition a new House Block was constructed incorporating six house rooms (which would be used for dining) associated teaching spaces and ancillary accommodation, including kitchens on the first floor, with additional teaching space, cloakrooms, toilets and a service area on the ground floor.

A new sports hall in the PE block measured 90ft by 55ft whilst a swimming pool 66ft by 24ft was also now provided.

In 1974 Acklam High School split to form Kings Manor 11-16 School and Acklam Sixth Form College, each occupying one of two new teaching blocks in front of the original Manor House, within which accommodation was shared.

The Kings Manor building suffered the fate of being destroyed by fire following which Kings Manor School moved across Hall Drive to the site shared with Hall Garth School. The block was finally demolished in 1997 leaving Acklam sixth form college as the sole occupant of the site.

Top: *Acklam Hall after extension in 1958.* ***Below left:*** *Longlands College after extensions in 1968.* ***Below:*** *Longlands Main Entrance, 1968.*

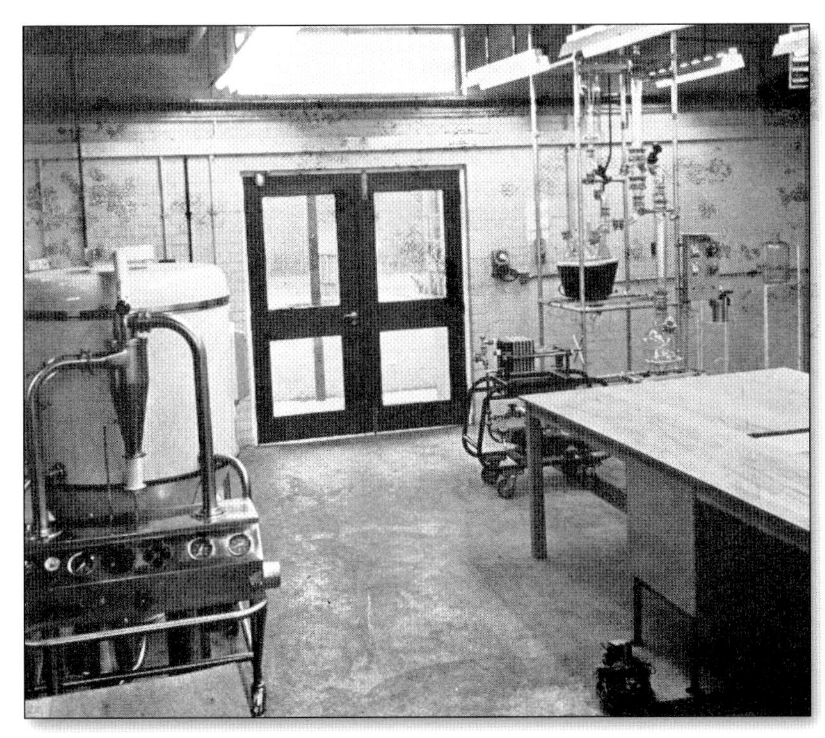

The College's buildings were situated on Douglas Street. On 27th November 1968 Mrs Shirley Williams MP, Minister of State for the Department of Education and Science, officially opened extensions to Longlands College of Further Education. The extensions which cost nearly £700,000 doubled the area of the buildings and included a new four-storey wing, workshops and a sports hall.

Additional class and laboratory provision was located in the new wing which was linked to the existing four-storey block and which, with the sports hall, communal and administrative accommodation, formed a courtyard served at each corner by a staircase.

Additional workshops were formed by double banking the existing workshop block and extending a U-shaped wing around the service road.

Meanwhile the development of further education in Middlesbrough was being determined by the growth of student numbers of Constantine College of Technology and its transformation from a centre of all vocational further education courses to an institution of higher education, initially as Teesside Polytechnic, and subsequently as the University of Teesside.

Decentralisation began in 1954 with the administrative and physical removal of Art courses from Constantine College (although the permanent College of Art building did not open until 1958). Pressure of numbers saw the use of large amounts of temporary accommodation in various parts of Middlesbrough, and it was a relief when in September 1958 Longlands College, on Douglas Street, opened as an annexe.

The administrative separation of Longlands College from its parent took place in September 1959, on the basis that Longlands would provide less advanced courses, with priority being given to engineering. In subsequent years the college would offer courses relevant to many of the local industries: chemical plant operation, pattern making, and foundry technology, electrical installation, instrumentation, telecommunications, motor vehicle mechanics, naval architecture, metallurgy and plumbing.

However the early Longlands College offered a much wider range of courses: a prospectus for 1961 indicates that under Principal Mr J Wood the College also offered courses in hairdressing, horticulture, bread making, cake decorations, and even courses for those wishing to train as dental technicians.

From September 1965 Longlands College was joined by another further education provider: Kirby College of Further Education.

Top left: *Longlands Chemistry Laboratory, 1968.* ***Below:*** *Sir Keith Jospeh Secretary of State for Education is shown around by the Principal Dr Tony Shaw on 11 June 1984.*

The Kirby College of Further Education was originally established in September 1965 as the West Middlesbrough College of Further Education. The nucleus of the new college had been created by the transfer from Constantine College of Technology of commercial, secretarial and GCE courses. In 1966 the College assumed responsibility for courses in breadmaking, hairdressing, pre-nursing and horticulture, which had previously been offered at the Longlands College of Further Education. In 1967 the Women's Educational Centre based in The Barns building on Orchard Road became the Department of Food and Fashion and was integrated into the College.

WHAT WE SEEK IS THE REIGN OF LAW BASED UPON THE CONSENT OF THE GOVERNED AND SUSTAINED BY THE ORGANISED OPINION OF MANKIND

THIS IS TO CERTIFY THAT THE LEAGUE OF NATIONS SOCIETY AT Kirby Secondary School Middlesbrough HAS BEEN DULY CONSTITUTED A SCHOOL BRANCH of the League of Nations Union under powers granted to the Union by its Royal Charter and under arrangements sanctioned by the Executive Committee for "Junior Branches." As witness the Seal of the Union is hereto affixed this 16th day of Dec: 1927 by order of the Executive Committee.

The Seal affixed in the presence of

Secretary

LEAGVE OF NATIONS UNION

The College was originally housed in the former Middlesbrough Girls High School building in King Edwards Road and in an annexe in Marton Grove. However it was always the intention that the College would occupy the premises vacated by Kirby Girls Grammar School on Roman Road.

The Kirby Secondary School on Roman Road was opened on 17th October 1911. The opening ceremony was performed by HRH Prince Arthur of Connaught, who that same day also opened the Transporter Bridge. The School subsequently became Kirby Girls Grammar School, and in 1967 moved to Acklam.

Top left: *A 1970s bird's eye view of the Kirby site with all extensions.* ***Centre:*** *A League of Nations certificate to certify Kirby Secondary School as a School Branch.* ***Right:*** *The Hairdressing Salon at Kirby College in 1972.*

From 1966 onwards the premises at Roman Road were extended to include a five-storey teaching block and a two storey communal block. In 1968 the premises were occupied by Kirby College of Further Education.

The pre-war single-storey classroom block facing Roman Road was however considered to be unsuitable for satisfactory alterations to meet the needs of the new College. The Department of Education and Science agreed with a proposal to demolish the original block and replace it with a much larger two-storey building. The new block would house the food and fashion departments and be linked to the main building and the drama block at both ground and first floors.

Additionally a new main entrance to the College was formed on the ground floor as a link between the old building and the new. The ground floor of the drama block was extended to provide extra cloakroom facilities adjacent to the students' common room.

A new wing including specialist catering, hairdressing, and office-practice facilities, as well as improved library and communal facilities was officially opened in September 1972 by the Lord Boyle of Handsworth. At this time the Principal was Mr GJ Edwards and the College accommodated 520 full-time, and 5,000 part-time, students.

Marton Sixth Form College was established on Marton Road in what had formerly been the premises of Middlesbrough High School.

Middlesbrough High School for Boys had been established in 1870 in Grange Road. A High School for Girls was opened in 1874. Both schools transferred to new buildings on King Edwards Road in 1877.

Extensions to Constantine College of Technology and a recognition that Victorian buildings were inappropriate for 20th

century education prompted a relocation in 1959 to new premises on Marton Road. In 1974 the premises became the base for Marton Sixth Form College.

During the latter part of the 20th century there were a number of significant developments for further education. The Further Education Act 1992 removed control of colleges from local authorities. In 1995 Longlands College merged with Marton Sixth Form College to create Teesside Tertiary College. At the same time Kirby College merged with Acklam Sixth Form College to form Middlesbrough College.

The present Middlesbrough College came into being on 1st August 2002 as the result of the merger of Middlesbrough College and Teesside Tertiary College.

Currently the Acklam campus is home to all AS and A2 Level study. The Marton campus is dedicated to Business, Creative Arts, Media, eMedia, ICT, Performing Arts, Music, Skills for Life, Sport & Recreation and Uniformed/Public Services. The

Longlands campus has Engineering, Construction and Motor Vehicle studies while Kirby is the base for all Health and Care, Catering and Hospitality, Travel and Tourism, and Hair and Beauty programmes.

Meanwhile the move to Middlehaven will itself be another reminder of the area's history. The new College will be located on the site of what was once a busy dock area.

The first dock was built at a cost of £122,558 (just under £6million at today's prices) and was opened on 12th May 1842. It was expanded and developed a number of times in subsequent years to accommodate growing traffic and the changed size of vessels using it. A Clock Tower has been a significant feature of the landscape since the beginning; though the current tower dates only from about 1870.

In the design of the new College the dock has provided inspiration, and the building will feature a 'hull' and a 'wave'. The building will face the dock, and the central street will have as a focal point the Clock Tower.

In the 21st century Middlesbrough College caters for the whole community. There are in excess of 13,000 students registered with the College ranging from 8-80 years of age. With hundreds of courses to choose from, students can learn at a time and place which fits in with every individual's lifestyle.

Top left: *In November 2007 Old Boys of Middlesbrough High School meet at Marton Campus to remember the 208 former staff and pupils who died in two world wars.* ***Above left:*** *The Marton Campus in 2007.* ***Top right:*** *Councillor Hazel Pearson, OBE, Chairman of the Governors and John Hogg, Principal, put their hand-prints in the new building at Middlehaven.* ***Below:*** *The new College emerges alongside the Dock and the Transporter Bridge, November 2007.*

David Fox Transport

Leading the Field with Commitment, Service and Quality

Folk who are keen on finding out the answer to puzzles may like to ponder the following question: what have Neil Armstrong (the first man on the moon), the rock band Genesis, and a model of a football stadium all got in common? The answer is that they have all been taken to their destinations by Middlesbrough's David Fox Transport!

David Fox Transport Ltd is a medium-sized, family-run business which holds dear the traditional business values of commitment, service and quality with which the company was established. It specialises in the transportation of steel, newsprint and non-hazardous chemicals throughout the UK, but can offer solutions to a great many other haulage and transport needs.

Today the business has two depots: one in Humberside and one in Teesside. The main office is located in the Tees Valley at Bolckow Road, Grangetown, Middlesbrough. Immingham, South Humberside is the location for satellite offices, and a second base for the firm's vehicles.

Founded by David William Fox in 1969, when he was just 18 years old, today the company owns and operates a mixed fleet of high quality vehicles. When starting up the business David was fortunate to be able to call on the advice and guidance of his father, Alexander Ballantyne Fox who had his own personal experience of the haulage industry, having worked for R Rankin & Son. It was Alex who negotiated with TDG plc, which owned R Rankin, permission for David to enter the transport arena on the condition that he did not go into direct competition with the Rankin business. Alex made another vital contribution to his son's fledgling business in the form of a £750 loan. That money enabled David to purchase second hand vans and mini buses to lease. It was given as a loan but Alex never asked for it back - though it must also be said that David never actually offered to repay it either!

Others too would be of great help: close family involvement has always been a feature of the company's story. In addition to Alex's initial input a further three generations have contributed to the success of the firm; David and his brother Richard, David's wife Alison, David's father-in-law Ted Veal and David's two sons, David (Jnr) and James.

At the outset however David worked alone, operating a van hire business and undertaking emergency express deliveries

***Top:** Founder David Fox. **Below left:** David Fox pictured in front of one of his first vans, 1970. **Below:** A David Fox van from the 1970s.*

of up to 1 tonne, working for Smiths Docks Co. Ltd at South Bank and Shell Oil at Teesport Refinery. At that time the business was based at the premises of R & I Raby on Snowdon Road, Middlesbrough, referred to by locals as 'Over the Border' until more suitable premises could be found. These were days involving long hours: David had to keep appointments and also try and increase the range of clients. But growth came very quickly.

The company had taken over the Acklam Road Service Station, next to the Coronation Hotel, in 1970. Here there was ample parking space as well as fuelling and servicing facilities for the light vans and commercial vehicles which David was operating at the time. A year later there was another move - to larger premises in Stonehouse Street, Linthorpe village. This was the year that David was able to acquire five articulated vehicles and trailers - these were kept and maintained at the old Andersons Foundry at Port Clarence. Since 1976 the company has been based at its present location, Bolckow Road, Grangetown. The satellite office was opened at Immingham on South Humberside in 1991, run by Don Rooney who had been with the firm since 1972.

The early 1970s were however to prove a baptism by fire for the fledgling firm.

In October 1973 two international crises – one economic, one political – combined with dramatic and long term consequences for businesses of all kinds - not least those involved in transport. On 6th October, Egypt and Syria both launched an attack on Israel, and within a few days the major Arab oil

Above: *David Fox outside his first garage, 1970.* ***Left:*** *David's sister Alison after learning to drive their 'Old Dolly' 1934 Baby Austin 7.*

producers announced their support by use of the 'oil weapon', including a boycott of supplies for countries friendly to Israel and a programme of production cuts. This was followed by the unilateral declaration of a steep increase in the price of oil by the Organization of Petroleum Exporting Countries (OPEC).

The consquence was international panic and world recession. Crude oil prices soared by a massive fourfold in just three months. The West's vulnerability had been exposed: it was being held hostage to oil. For a while petrol rationing became a real possibility in Britain. In the following years, despite efforts to address this dependence on oil imports, the 1979 Iranian Revolution triggered a further upward surge in prices. As the price of diesel rose and the British economy moved towards slump many firms folded. Yet despite these challenges David Fox and his company survived, and not merely survived but prospered.

In 1979 a significant development occurred when an Executive Coach business was launched. This brought David's sister, Alison into the firm. Following the success of this new line of business David's brother, Richard joined the company in 1983. Richard, who was 19 at the time, had been an apprentice footballer with Middlesbrough during the reigns of Jack Charlton, John Neil and Bobby Murdoch.

It was under Jack Charlton that Middlesbrough Football Club became Second Division Champions. To celebrate the occasion David Fox Transport provided a tractor unit and a 40ft trailer made up to look like a football pitch. Unfortunately the level of excitement in the local population increased to such an extent that the trailer had to be taken away when boys started climbing on it as it was parked outside the Evening Gazette offices.

The company acquired a chassis cab through Bill Beadnell of Brian Sharp DAF Trucks Ltd, Billingham and arranged for the manufacture of a special body and interior for it by Van Hool Ltd, Europe's principal coach builders. On

***Above:** Enjoying a glass of bubbly, David Fox (left), Nigel Shaw, David's wife Alison and David's sister Alison (far right). **Below:** A David Fox award winning coach of 1979.*

completion in 1979, the coach was presented at the 25th Annual Coach of the Year Show at Brighton and won the 'Coach of the Year Award' along with several other silver jubilee trophies. The coach was the first of a new breed in coach travel and made possible an entirely new experience for coach passengers. Only those who have travelled long distances on uncomfortable, cramped coaches with nothing better to do than try and read magazines until the next coffee stop, could fully appreciate the revolutionary nature of this first class coach.

That vehicle having been acquired at great cost, the firm was able to offer a first class service for travelling celebrities, and that is how Neil Armstrong and Genesis came to be transported on David Fox coaches. This led to another exciting development when the firm secured contracts to be involved in the movement of staging and scaffolding equipment for European tours of music groups such as the Rolling Stones, Genesis, Bruce Springsteen, Queen and Michael Jackson. One such contract was with a group called John Watts and Para Music - a happy coincidence as John Watts was also the name of the man who drove the coaches for many years, and who played his own special part in the success of the company.

David Fox Transport has always made a priority of being equipped with an up-to-date and well maintained fleet. New vehicles are regularly purchased to replace older ones.

Throughout its history, commitment, service, quality and training have been the core values behind the company's success. Those values will also form the bedrock of future developments. The company has been awarded the prestigious BS EN ISO 9002:1994 accreditation. All their

vehicles are serviced regularly in-house by their skilled fitting staff who man the Grangetown depot 24 hours a day, Monday to Saturday. All long distance vehicles are equipped with 'In-Cab' communications equipment and some drivers are trained in Hazpack regulations. Transport managers, operators and office staff all have a comprehensive, long-standing knowledge of the industry and can instantly help with any distribution problems. Alongside those previously mentioned are other long-serving staff members such as Nancy Truran, Company Secretary, who joined the firm in

Top left: *David Fox Trailer unit made up as a football pitch to celebrate Middlesbrough's Second Division Championship.* ***Above:*** *David Fox Transport advertised at a 1980s match between Middlesbrough and Ipswich Town.* ***Left:*** *Richard Kirby, Accountant (left) and Alex Fox Managing Director and Chairman of Cleveland Tankers Ltd.*

1972, around the same time as Don Rooney. Both Nancy and Don are good friends of the Fox Family. Barry Mitchell, who served his apprenticeship with David Fox Transport, Charles Dryden, Bill Filer, Linda Stockell, Pauline Taggart and Dawn Hoggarth, and some long-serving drivers such as John Cubbin, Brian Thompson, Ged Stebulitis, Terry Barker and Reg Gant to name but a few.

Transport has not been the only area in which the company has developed its services. There is always an ongoing need for training, and David Fox Transport has its own facilities offering individual training courses for forklift trucks, gantry cranes and other relevant topics. These courses are open to the general public and other businesses. The facilities have been used by other hauliers, crane and

engineering companies and local councils. The company's philosophy is to grow steadily and maintain a good customer base built on reliability of service without resorting to cut price tactics in a shrinking marketplace.

This philosophy has stood the firm in good stead over the years and has led to the success which it enjoys today. It has helped the company weather some major storms over the years, in particular the closure of two of its main customers in the Middlesbrough area, namely Shell UK at the Teesport Refinery and Smith Docks Ltd at South Bank and Haverton Hill. Since these closures there has also been the virtual end of ICI Billingham and the closure of several steel plants as well as the changes at ICI Wilton. But enjoying a wide customer base the firm looks set for continuing success in the future.

Today the company is involving itself with more 'High Street' oriented activities. This has necessitated investment.

Top right: *A Fox heavy goods vehicle.* ***Above:*** *The crew of the 'Rolling Stones' tour.* ***Right:*** *A montage of the David Fox workshop.*

The Company took on the distribution of profiles steel plate for Corus at Leeds in 2002. This involved an expansion, with five extra vehicles and ten trailers being placed at their disposal. The company was engaged in distributing Corus' finished products and also bringing in most of the steel plate and coil for the various processes. Additional business was won in the Scunthorpe and South Yorkshire area giving the company loads to convey back to the North East, thereby completing a circle.

Teesport has also played an important part over the last few years, seeing an increase in the import of forest products. More recently has been the introduction of ASDA Walmart to the Teesport success story. ASDA Walmart has opened an import centre for goods from all over the world, and David Fox Transport has been fortunate to capture some of that

business. This involved further investment in additional equipment, particularly double deck trailers for lightweight goods, maximising the (two loads for one) space. The company's presence on Humberside is strong and mirrors the position at Teesport as an expanding area. Indeed the Northeast coast is becoming the future for inland trade, in and out.

Young David Fox Jnr, and now James, fresh from serving his apprenticeship in the Workshop, have now entered the company's Traffic Office under the watchful eye of their Uncle Richard. Another new starter as a Traffic Co-ordinator in the Traffic Office is Daniel Lund. David Jnr has stepped into Bill Filer's shoes after his retirement in 2005 although Bill still works two or three days each week. According to his father James is learning his trade well and when needed, can turn his hand to driving.

Richard's wife Linda is now playing more of an active role in the company now that their two boys, Daniel and Liam, 'aspiring footballers' both of them, are growing up. The company has tentative plans for the future, bearing in mind the change of direction that the country as a whole is taking.

Vehicle maintenance plays a big part in the operation of any transport company and Charles Dryden and his team ensure the fleet of vehicles, presently 65 Tractor

Units and 130 Trailers are kept well maintained and on the road.

Linda Stockell, Christine Walker and Denise Sill make sure the bills go out on time. Nancy Truran, 35 years with the Company and Pauline Taggart, 25 years with the Company ensure the bills are paid. Altogether, a fine line-up.

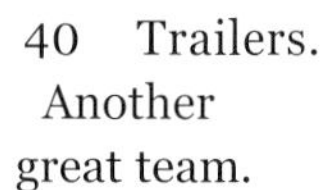

Barry Eastham and his team at Immingham play an integral part in the organisation in the DFDS Torline Terminal on Humberside looking after 20 Tractor Units and 40 Trailers. Another great team.

Today, with its superb staff, the future of David Fox Transport Ltd is as bright as its past.

Top left: *David Fox with wife Alison and Sons David Jnr (left) and James, 2001.* ***Top left inset:*** *David Fox being presented with the keys to the first four Iveco Ford Tractor Units to enter the David Fox Transport Fleet. The presentation was made by Bill Beadnell, Chairman of North East Truck and Van Ltd.* ***Far left:*** *Daniel Lund.* ***Top right:*** *David Fox Transport and Asda double deck trailers.* ***Above centre:*** *The David Fox Transport admin team.* ***Above right:*** *Barry Eastham.* ***Below:*** *The next generation, Richard Fox (left), James Fox (centre) and David Fox.*

University of Teesside
Constant To The Constantine Vision

How many readers have fond memories of evening classes or daytime courses at what is now the University of Teesside? This educational institution based on a single site in the centre of Middlesbrough has been serving the needs of local residents and of local industry for over seventy years. During that time it has undergone a number of name changes, as well as changes to the type of course it offers, but the University is fulfilling the same purpose the College has fulfilled throughout its history.

Although the need to create an institution in Middlesbrough to provide advanced education in technical and commercial subjects had been recognised in the late 1800s, the origins of the University of Teesside lie in the vision and extreme generosity of a local shipping magnate, Joseph Constantine. His attitude is well illustrated in part of the speech he made to the education committee in 1916: 'I have been identified with Middlesbrough the whole of my commercial life, and I have always felt that I should like to do something that might be of benefit to the community...We have been moving in very serious times lately, and it appears to all that when the time of peace comes we must be properly equipped to stand up against the very serious competition we must expect from other countries, including Germany.' The

***Top:** The original Constantine Building, 1930.* ***Above left:** Joseph Constantine.* ***Above:** A collection of Constantine College Brochures from the 1930s and 1950s.*

This was an astronomical sum at the time and it made the building of the technical college in what is now the Constantine Building of the University on the junction of Borough Road and Albert Road possible.

From then until the late 1960s Constantine College provided a mix of further and higher education technical and commercial courses. Despite the economic difficulties of the time the College grew steadily with about 2,000, mainly part-time evening, students attending by the outbreak of the second world war.

The war inevitably saw a drop in the number of its students but Constantine College still provided vital training and educational services to the essential war industries of the region. One vital function was provision of technical

committee had no hesitation in accepting with gratitude the generosity of their benefactor.

Between 1916 and the formal opening of the college named after him by the then Prince of Wales in July 1930 Constantine donated over £80,000 to the enterprise.

This page: *The opening of Constantine College by the then Prince of Wales, July 1930.*

training for the many women who came into local industries to replace the men conscripted into the armed forces.

The College even engaged in the production of specialist equipment for local firms during the war.

In the early post-war years, the College, which was already being overwhelmed by the growth of numbers before the outbreak of war, found itself in some difficulty to meet the great expansion in educational demands. With virtually no investment in buildings or equipment during the war the College struggled to accommodate the rising demand for places on its courses, especially with the growth of day release of young workers for educational purposes. What many before the war had seen as primarily an evening class centre became mainly a day college as the number of full-time students also increased. At the same time the number of students on full-time and sandwich externally validated degree courses in subjects such as engineering, metallurgy and chemistry expanded and shifted the balance between further and higher education.

This shift led in the mid 1950s to a belief that the college should gain recognition as a College of Advanced Technology, one of eight that the Government was planning to create. This attempt to boost the status of the College was ultimately unsuccessful, but it signalled a desire by the College and its controlling local education authority that it should become the basis of a fully-fledged institution of higher education.

By 1960 there were over five and a half thousand students, many still attending part-time evening classes. However, the crisis in accommodation had only been tackled by the construction of temporary buildings and by making use of secondary school premises and equipment in the evenings.

During the 1960s the College offered seventeen degree courses under the auspices of the new validating authority the Council for National Academic Awards. The narrow technical and commercial orientation of the College was broadened to include Liberal Studies in the humanities and social sciences.

This page: *New and old pictures of the Waterhouse Building.*

After the creation of the unified Teesside local authority there developed a campaign for the creation of a university in the area and most importantly as far as Constantine College was concerned its designation as a polytechnic. This development meant that degrees with a strongly vocational character could be offered.

It was about this time that the chronic shortage of suitable accommodation was addressed; the old High School buildings had been acquired and the highly visible eleven-storey tower block built.

In 1970, Constantine College was formally redesignated Teesside Polytechnic and its status as an institution of higher education clarified, though many locally still referred to it as Constantine College. The creation of the Polytechnic led to the development of plans for a huge expansion of the site and increased student numbers. These plans were, however, dogged by rather difficult relations with the local authorities, now split between the district of Middlesbrough responsible for planning, and the county of Cleveland the controlling education authority. There was also a current of feeling in some local political circles that the Polytechnic stood in the way of the creation of a university on Teesside.

Above and left: *By day and by night views of the Centuria Building. Opened in 2000 the building houses the School of Health and Social Care, a 21st century state-of-the-art centre for the fast growing academic area on Teesside.* ***Below:*** *The Innovation Centre, also home to the School of Science & Technology.*

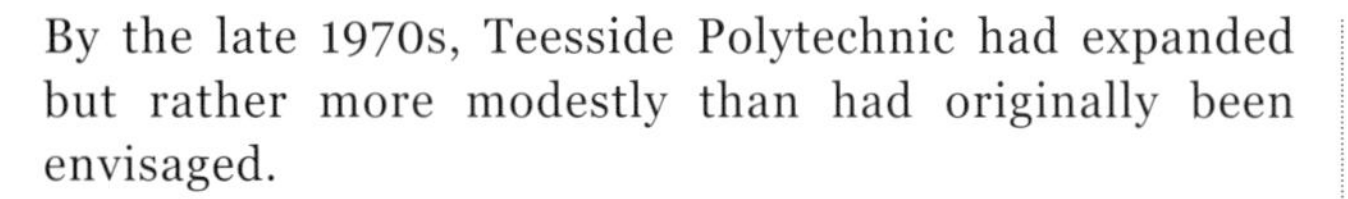

By the late 1970s, Teesside Polytechnic had expanded but rather more modestly than had originally been envisaged.

In line with Government policy, which was to sever links between the local education authorities and the polytechnics, Teesside gained independent corporate status in 1989. Middlesbrough then at long last became a university town in 1992 when the polytechnic became the University of Teesside. Since then the campus has changed dramatically with the building of new halls of residence, an award-winning Learning Resource Centre and a new School of Health and Social Care building. In fact, health is now the largest of the six

Top left and above: *The Learning Resource Centre. Opened in 1997 the centre provides students with a full range of top quality facilities to support their studies. Being one of the best of its kind in the university sector students are able to use a full range of information sources from books to the web.*
Below: *Teesside University's Olympia Building.*

schools in the University. The two most recent developments have been the Phoenix and Athena buildings on Woodlands Road where undergraduate and postgraduate students can study at the very cutting edge of digital technology and at the same time make very real contributions to the economic regeneration of the Tees Valley region.

Technology remains important with over 2,500 students on science and technology courses, but even more are involved in computing and other information technology courses, undertaking studies beyond the imagination of the founders of Constantine College in 1930. Now, students at Teesside can study virtual reality, physiotherapy, sport and exercise, media studies, forensic science, law, graphic design, public relations or local modern and medieval history to name just a very few of the undergraduate and postgraduate, full and part-time programmes now available at the University. The University is also making a major contribution to the cultural growth of the area with new programmes of study in fine art, benefiting from such close proximity to Middlesbrough's iconic Institute of Modern Art (MIMA), and also in the performing arts.

A major employer in its own right, and seen by government and the regional development agency as pivotal in the economic regeneration of the Tees Valley area, the founders of Constantine College would undoubtedly be proud that their creation had, almost three quarters of a century later, become an institution of 24,000 students equipped to meet the educational and professional development needs of the people of Teesside in a way appropriate to the changing industrial and economic climate.

Left: *The Athena Building.* ***Top:*** *The Phoenix Building.* ***Below:*** *By night view of the Tower and Waterhouse Building.*

PD Ports - Teesport

Located on the North East coast of England is Teesport, part of PD Ports and one of the UK's three busiest maritime ports by volume of annual cargoes. Teesport employs over 550 staff and is the natural gateway to the North of the UK for shippers. Today the Port consistently handles more than 50 million tonnes and 6,000 ship arrivals per annum.

Teesport, which includes Hartlepool Dock, is one of Britain's oldest and most important ports. There has been significant port operations on the River Tees in North East England since the 12th Century.

The Port became commercially important when it first developed at a river crossing point on the trade route between Durham and York. The main port was originally at Yarm and vessels of up to 65 tonnes would sail the 23 miles upstream. At that time there was considerable trade with Flanders, France and Scotland.

In 1770, Yarm river traffic was cut off from Stockton following the construction of the low level Victoria Bridge in the town. This resulted in the shipping trade moving down river to Stockton.

With the mining of local coal and the discovery of iron ore in the 1800s, traffic increased and led to the construction of the local Stockton to Darlington railway. So in 1826, the railway was extended to Port Darlington, or Middlesbrough as it is known today, and activity moved closer to the mouth of the river. By 1871 the population of Teesside was 215,535 and the region at this time was the world's major steel production centre.

As the town of Middlesbrough continued to grow and activities on the river increased, Middlesbrough dock was opened in 1842 with a capacity of 150 ships. During

Above and below: *Then and now. A 1897 view of the river Tees and a 2007 view of Tees Dock.* ***Right:*** *A post war bird's eye view of Middlesbrough dock.*

the 20th Century the Port saw continued growth of coal and steel shipments as well as being home to an important shipbuilding industry. The Port was repeatedly attacked by German planes during the Second World War. The railway station at Middlesbrough and buildings around PD Ports' head office at Queen's Square suffered considerable damage.

During the mid 1950s plans were crystallised to transform the North bank of the Tees by a major land reclamation from the marshy estuary. This area, known as Seal Sands developed during the 1970s and is today Europe's second largest complex of processing plants for oils and chemicals.

On the South side the discovery and opening up of North Sea oil and gas fields saw the development of the Tees Offshore Park for fabrication of oil rigs and platforms, plus mooring for their subsequent supply vessels. The North Sea oil and gas coming ashore in two pipelines at the mouth of the Tees has seen some decline in recent years and so this old shipbuilding area of Smiths Dock has been renamed again.

Known today as Tees Commerce Park, it is home to several logistics operators as well as continuing to act as a supply base for North Sea platforms and more recently for an offshore wind farm installation vessel. The port area around the Tees has long been renowned for its ability to rejuvenate itself and find new cargoes and commercial activities.

In 1980 Middlesbrough dock closed and was later renamed as Middlehaven in the 1990s. Today the area around Middlehaven is home to premier football team Middlesbrough at their Riverside Stadium and is undergoing a massive regeneration programme of work with offices and a new college of further education.

Due to the major growth of shipping traffic during the industrial revolution of the 19th Century, the Tees Conservancy Commissioners, the founders of a major part of the origins of PD Ports, were formed in 1852. The Commissioners headquarters were initially based in Stockton, only to relocate to Middlesbrough's Queen's Square in 1899. The headquarters remains at Queen's Square to this day.

Eight miles downriver from Queen's Square is Tees Dock, which was constructed and opened in 1965/66. It was in this year that an Act of Parliament established Tees and Hartlepool Port Authority as the controlling body for the river.

As a consequence of the abolition of the National Dock Labour Board Scheme in 1989 the Port was privatised in 1992. The original three joint buyers in 1992 were then subsequently, reduced to a single owner, Powell Duffryn plc, by 1995. This stock exchange listed company was then itself taken over in 2000 by private Japanese owned banking group Nikko and its various maritime and port businesses re-branded in 2003 as PD Ports, Logistics and Shipping (PDPLS). In December 2004, the company, PD Ports plc, was listed on the London AIM stock market and was successfully taken over by Australian investment firm, Babcock and Brown Infrastructure (BBI) in February 2006 to form PD Ports Limited.

TEESPORT - TODAY

Today, Teesport is a thriving ports business, consistently handling more than 50 million tonnes and 6,000 ship arrivals each year. The award winning port is one of the largest employers in North East England and has the vision to further expand and develop, seeking world class status across the business.

The Port continues to build upon its strong relationships with the petrochemicals, engineering and manufacturing industries. Local petrochemical and steel industries drive large volumes of traffic through Teesport but cars and general bulk cargoes such as potash are also very important.

In 2006 ASDA Wal*Mart opened a new import centre at Teesport. The 350,000 sq ft facility handles ASDA's general merchandise destined for the retailer's Northern retail stores and consumers. As a result of establishing its base at Teesport, ASDA will save up to 2 million road miles each year on UK inland distribution and significantly reduce its CO2 emissions. Teesport is firmly committed to facilitating such significant environmental benefits through further such import centre developments in the future.

2007 saw even bigger changes with the arrival of the world's first dockside regasification facility at Teesport. Excelerate Energy opened the Teesside GasPort facility to handle liquefied natural gas (LNG). This process involves shipments of LNG aboard Excelerate Energy's specially designed Energy Bridge vessels, which allow LNG to be revaporized to gas onboard the ships. When docked at Teesport, the gas can then be fed into the National Transmission System.

TEESPORT – THE FUTURE

Over recent years, market changes have seen a further shift in traffic with a decrease in the handling of traditional cargoes such as finished steel and a rapid growth of both intermediate steel such as slabs and of container handling. The world's container shipping market will continue to grow, fuelled by the boom in Far East manufacturing, particularly growing imports from China.

The strategic location of Teesport and its deep water capability means it is a vital trading link with mainland European and global markets. As part of its future growth strategy, PD Ports has exciting plans to build a £300 million deep sea container terminal on the South side of the River Tees. It is envisaged that The Northern Gateway Container Terminal will open up additional opportunities for trade with the Far East and elsewhere.

The Northern Gateway will bring over 5,500 much needed jobs to North East England, attracting retailers and others to develop import/distribution centres at Teesport. The project will also help address the economic disparity between the North and South and will be a major catalyst in regenerating the economy of North East England.

Top left: *Queen's Street headquarters pictured in the 1960s.* ***Below left:*** *A recent interior view of the Queen's Square boardroom.* ***Below:*** *An aerial shot of Teesport in 2007. Outlined is where The Northern Gateway Container Terminal will be built.*

Emanuel Spence - Still Giving Careful Attention

Heating, plumbing, electrical works, building, and glazing. Middlesbrough's Emanuel Spence Ltd seems to offer everything – all the old skills plus several new tricks too.

Emanuel Spence (pictured left) was born in 1868, and was one of nine children.

In 1891 Emanuel Spence married Ann Newbould a daughter of the Newbould butchery family. Ann however died in 1915 and Emanuel married Florence Almgill (below right) in 1916. The Almgill family were responsible for building many of the properties in central Middlesbrough. Florence Almgill was one of four sisters, Maude, Hilda and Freda being the others. Florence, Maude, Hilda and Freda had already been well provided for on their 21st birthdays as each had each been given a substantial block of terraced properties. In 1949 Florence owned 39 properties comprising of most of Craven Street, Talbot Street, Roscoe Street and Falkland Street.

Maude did not marry; Hilda however married Albert Forbes who founded the Forbes bakery chain and was responsible for Forbes Buildings a prominent feature of Linthorpe Road even now. Freda married Marcus Mcnay who founded Mcnays steel who went on to be part of GKN.

Emanuel Spence founded his plumbing business in 1895.

Emanuel had started his first shop in 1906 – a fact recorded in the 1906 Park Wesleyan Church bazaar magazine. He was a prominent Methodist and a local preacher. Those Methodist roots followed him into business: his motto for the day was: 'Careful attention given to all orders'.

Aldermen
Councillors
Thanks to the retiring Mayor and Mayoress
Mayor
Town Clerk

In 1910 Emanuel became a councillor of the Acklam ward. He was elected to be Mayor in 1919 - the Town Council commissioned a specially painted scroll (above) to thank him for his work - the only one ever undertaken.

Florence Spence, Middlesbrough's first Lady Mayoress, was also Middlesbrough's first lady driver! (Below left).

One of the major projects undertaken by Middlesbrough council's Sanitary Department in 1926, was the installation of modern water closets. The Master Plumbers' Association was called in and a price for each conversion was agreed at 48s 6d.

Emanuel Spence, one of the best-known plumbers in the town and a forthright councillor, did his own sums and concluded that the ratepayers were being taken for a ride. Although he stood to lose out personally the cost of each conversion was finally reduced to 15s.6d. His intervention did not go down well with the other plumbing contractors on the job!

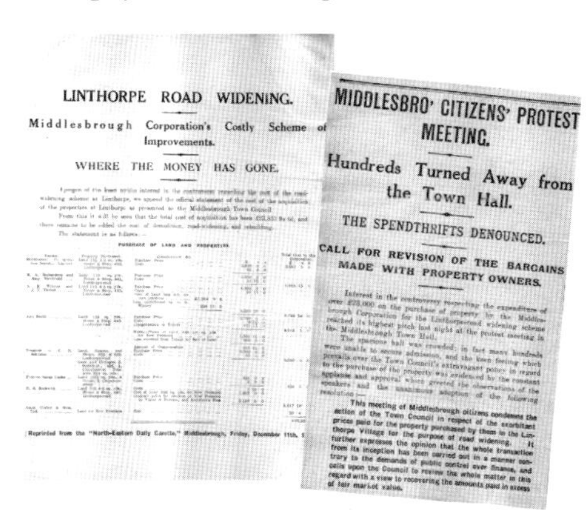

LINTHORPE ROAD WIDENING.

Middlesbrough Corporation's Costly Scheme of Improvements.

WHERE THE MONEY HAS GONE.

Reprinted from the "North-Eastern Daily Gazette," Middlesbrough, Friday, December 11th,

MIDDLESBRO' CITIZENS' PROTEST MEETING.

Hundreds Turned Away from the Town Hall.

THE SPENDTHRIFTS DENOUNCED.

CALL FOR REVISION OF THE BARGAINS MADE WITH PROPERTY OWNERS.

Interest in the controversy respecting the expenditure of over £23,000 on the purchase of property by the Middlesbrough Corporation for the Linthorpe-road widening scheme reached its highest pitch last night at the protest meeting in the Middlesbrough Town Hall.

The spacious hall was crowded; in fact many hundreds were unable to secure admission, and the keen feeling which prevails over the Town Council's extravagant policy in regard to the purchase of the property was evidenced by the constant applause and approval which greeted the observations of the speakers and the unanimous adoption of the following resolution:—

This meeting of Middlesbrough citizens condemns the action of the Town Council in respect of the exorbitant prices paid for the property purchased by them in the Linthorpe Village for the purpose of road widening. It further expresses the opinion that the whole transaction from its inception has been carried out in a manner contrary to the demands of public control over finance, and calls upon the Council to review the whole matter in this regard with a view to recovering the amounts paid in excess of fair market value.

Between 1924 and 1926 the great scheme was carried out to create a main road through the centre of Middlesbrough. To great protests from some quarters Emanuel ensured that this was carried out and at good value for money (above). In 1926 the people who ran Middlesbrough had a clear vision as to how the Town should look, today Middlesbrough needs that vision again. Few Councillors or Mayors since have come close to making such radical changes to improve the Town or been willing to stand up for such major projects.

Emanuel Spence died in 1948 - the company received over 300 letters of condolence.

The second generation of the company had arrived in 1917 with the birth of David Edward Spence. David was educated at Ashville College at Harrogate. David Spence went on to marry Doreen Horseman in 1952 and had two daughters, Anne and Jane. However as soon as he had come out of his apprenticeship in 1939 war was declared. David joined the Green Howards Regiment (below), he fought in France and was rescued at Dunkirk; he then served with the Eighth Army under Montgomery in the Middle East. Mentioned in Despatches twice David, seen below left taking the Salute in front of the Middlesbrough Town Hall, left the forces with the rank of Major. David Spence re-joined the company after discharge from the Green Howards.

One of the significant purchases after the second world war had been the acquisition in 1946 of the oldest glazing firm in Middlesbrough R Scupham & Sons, established in 1861. The original Scupham & Son premises were sold in 1952 and the business moved to a new site at 23/25 Dundas Street.

Emanuel Spence Ltd had occupied premises at 298 Linthorpe Road (left) from the early 1930s.

It was not until the early 1960s, after the sale of the Dundas Street site to make way for the new shopping development, that 300 Linthorpe Road was also occupied.

Meanwhile, in 1958, a time when much was changing, John David Spence, the firm's current Managing Director, had been born.

Whilst gas had been introduced for lighting and even for some early cookers in 1925 the majority of homeowners were still using coal fires for heating with back boilers for hot water. Companies such as The Beeston Boiler Company and The Ideal Boiler Company of Hull were introducing coal and coke fired boilers for domestic use.

On 17th May 1961 however, David Spence received the first domestic delivery of heating oil in Middlesbrough (below). The dirty chore of cleaning out the fireplace each day was banished, there was no more running to fetch coal, the drudgery of dusting was gone, and throughout the home there was an all over feeling of warmth and hospitality...if only!

In reality a house usually smelt of oil, servicing was a messy dirty business and occasionally the new 'state of the art heating boiler' would decide to explode and cover the garden in oily soot!

By the 1960s gas was discovered in the North Sea. In 1967 the conversion to North Sea gas was well underway bringing clean cheap central heating to millions.

John Spence (below) came into the business in 1980 as a result of David Spence's ill health. John attended St Peter's School in York, followed by Manchester University which resulted in a First Class degree in Electrical Engineering and Electronics.

John offered his father an excellent deal. David could retire, keep his salary and have a new car every three years and John would keep the balance. Little did John know there was no balance!

The premises had been rented for many years from another family member; working practices were still firmly grounded in the 1950s.

Re-building the business John's first task was to save up to buy the Linthorpe Road premises. By 1984 John had bought the premises which were altered and turned into a showroom and a bathroom shop (above).

The 1980s were very busy times: vandalism in Middlesbrough was at its height and Monday mornings were a glaziers paradise - every Monday up to four or five very large plate glass windows were being renewed. Several large prestigious works were also being completed such as the refurbishment of Grinkle Park Hotel.

The Company by this time had bought a fleet of vehicles, and even one of the new computers which had just come out.

Just as the business was growing again the recession of 1990 to 1992 arrived. However John Spence decided that this presented an opportunity when a local building company closed down on Letitia Industrial Estate. Just as the Agent's were putting up the signboard John put an offer into the receivers and it was accepted. The business moved there to its present premises (below) at Letitia Industrial Estate. John also sold his new car and bought new vans.

One of the significant changes of the 1990s for Emanuel Spence was offering a full multi trade service. People were no longer prepared to just employ a plumber or glazier, then wait for the joiner or bricklayer.

John Spence decided he should employ these trades directly and began by buying a small building company Ayresome Properties whose staff were now amalgamated into Emanuel Spence. Qualified electricians too completed the full compliment of trades.

John Spence too got a personal new recruit when he married Joanne Bolton on 9th December 2000.

Emanuel Spence has always looked to the future, and today is no exception.

And the future will be solar. Emanuel Spence Ltd has now invested in a new solar training facility and underfloor heating training room.

Most hot water at the firm is solar heated; its training room is lit by a 'Sunscoop' which provides free lighting.

Like his father and grandfather John Spence believes he should test all new products first before selling them to his

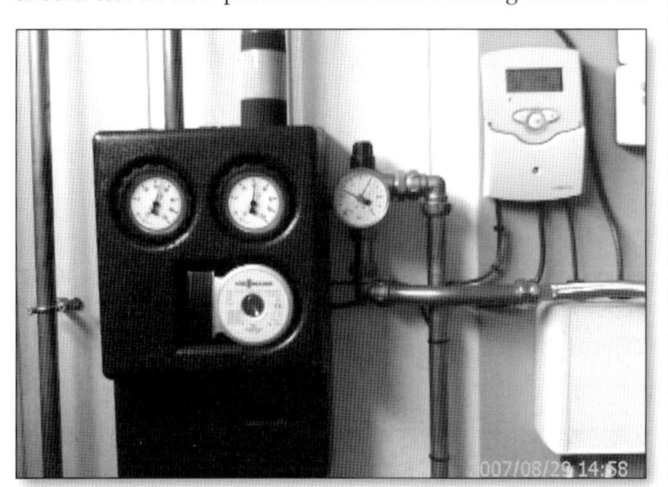

customers. John has installed the very latest in solar heating panels (above and below) from Viessmann in Germany, though not without a battle to gain planning permission.

New technology such as ground source heat pumps and heat recovery units which will redistribute heat in large buildings are also part of an energy conscious future. Lighting and power will come from photovoltaic power.

Yet whatever the future holds customers can still be assured that even after more than a century in business 'careful attention is still being given to all orders' by Emanuel Spence Ltd.

The Mall, Middlesbrough, - Decades of Endeavour

Today The Mall, Middlesbrough, is the largest shopping centre located in the heart of Middlesbrough and includes stores such as HMV, Boots, and Bhs. The centre has recently undergone a multi million pound development, which has seen the addition of stores such as New Look, Top Shop , George and H&M, making The Mall the premier retail destination for everyone's shopping needs.

In November 1961 property developers Norbert Sharland and Leslie Furness visited Middlesbrough to assess the possibilities of redevelopment there on a major scale. Neither knew the area well, so they spent many hours walking the town, watching the pedestrian flow, debating the merits of working on one site rather than another.

The main shopping thoroughfare was found to be so well-established that redevelopment away from that central core would have been foolish. The two men decided on the area bounded by Linthorpe Road, Bottomley Street, Fletcher Street and Fallows Street which seemed a typical and 'natural' area for shopping renewal and extension, absorbing the less valuable parts to the rear of Linthorpe Road to compensate for some of the very expensive property that would need to be bought on Linthorpe Road itself. As a result the established pedestrian flow through Newton Street would be maintained on redevelopment.

A meeting was held with the Borough Engineer and Surveyor. Messrs Sharland and Furness had already carefully investigated the commercial and social requirements of the project and made detailed financial plans to fund the work. It was time to call in the architects. They appointed Messrs Turner, Lansdowne, Holt and Partners, then, in the following year, set about private negotiations with the current owners of the properties they would need to acquire.

Within a few months the pair had negotiated contracts to buy several important properties. Now they needed to 'sell' their idea for development to a finance company willing to lend the

Below: *Construction of the Cleveland Centre begins in 1970.* ***Top right and below right:*** *Exterior views of the Cleveland Centre in the 1980s and 90s.*

estimated £3 million needed to make it happen. In due course an investment company, Barratt-Victoria (Middlesbrough) Property Company Ltd was formed.

Barratt-Victoria had a strong team. Its architects were sensitive to what would blend in well with the surrounding area of town. The company was also sensible enough to produce ideas that could be afforded financially, and experienced enough to cope with all the constructional problems. It was expected that rebuilding would begin within two to three years.

The Borough Engineer and Surveyor approved the plans submitted in April 1962, but they wanted the scheme enlarged to include Albert Road. Their suggestion was adopted; following which the scheme was further enlarged to co-ordinate with plans to rebuild between Wesley Street and Fallows Street. By March 1963 the Arndale Property Trust had submitted plans for a mammoth £10 million scheme stretching from Borough Road to Corporation Road. Perhaps feeling that the idea had grown too big, Barratt-Victoria submitted a third scheme and consultants were appointed to help make the final decision.

After several meetings, it was decided that Barratt-Victoria and Arndale would each proceed independently to develop the sites each owned, but all in conformity with the recommendations of the consultant surveyors. This co-operation seemed sensible since the substantial ownership of property already established would involve the minimum use of compulsory purchase powers.

However, it was not to be. The council decided it wished to deal with a single company or consortium as developer, and wanted unified ownership of the whole area. At this stage

Arndale now decided not to pursue the scheme it had submitted the previous year.

It was not until the summer of 1965, after Turner, Lansdowne, Holt & Partners had produced several variations on their plans that the council felt able to agree in principle to the scheme. The redevelopment area by now extended to six acres. The council intended to become the ground landlord, but private enterprise would acquire by agreement the multitude of other property interests. Public roads ran through the site which would have to be closed, and so it now became necessary to compulsorily acquire the land.

The compulsory purchasing involved exacting and time-consuming procedures under the Town and Country Planning Act. Numerous detailed plans were prepared, together with documents and reports. It was almost Christmas 1966 before the local authority formally submitted its proposals to the Minister of Housing and Local Government.

The necessary public enquiry was held in September 1967. A public exhibition had been held previously and affected traders had been promised rehousing in the scheme with continuity of trading wherever possible. There were therefore few objections and the Minister's approval to go ahead was given in 1968.

Promises to traders were kept. For example, the old Erimus public house was not demolished before new licensed premises were put up for Vaux Breweries and the National Westminster Bank was temporarily rehoused.

Building operations eventually started in July 1969. Six streets made way for the Cleveland Centre but these were not forgotten. The top half of Fletcher Street became the entrance to the centre for service vehicles to the first floor, and for shoppers' cars going to the second floor parking area. Two of the climate-controlled shopping malls would be named after Newton and Wesley Streets.

The original development took ten years from conception to completion at a cost of four million pounds. Construction was in three phases, the first opening in 1970 and covering some Linthorpe Road perimeter shops. In 1972 the second phase began with the opening of Newton Mall for the benefit of one shop: others however quickly followed. On completion of the third phase in 1973 there were 318,000 square feet of retail in a total 494,180 square feet.

By the early 1980s it was clear that the Centre had become outdated through normal wear and tear and changes of legislation concerning fire, health and safety. It was now that the Legal and General Assurance Company purchased the Centre.

In September 2004 the Cleveland Shopping Centre was bought by The Mall Corporation, the country's leading owner and developer of community shopping centres.

Shortly after the purchase The Mall embarked on a major multi-million pound development which included the reconfiguration of the Cleveland Square and the development of the former Littlewoods department store. In total 80,000 square foot of retail space was developed, successfully attracting new retailers to the town for the first time. As part of the development the owners also took the opportunity improve the internal decorations and facilities which helped attract a host of new retailers and customers.

In October 2006 The Mall bought the rights to the operate the 17,000 square metre roof top car park and proceeded to completely redevelop it, including resurfacing the entire area. Now the car park provides modern and safe facilities for all visitors to the mall and the town.

Legal and General appointed Bradshaw, Rowse and Harker as architects for the refurbishment programme carried out during 1984-6. It added 7,000 square feet of new retail space at a cost of more than £7 million. The Centre then consisted of 86 units incorporating a wine bar, restaurants, a roof top nightclub, three office blocks, a very large Health Centre and a car park with 550 spaces, leased to the local authority. In 1997 Legal and General again commissioned Bradshaw, Rowse and Harker to give the Centre a cosmetic uplift to the value of £3.5 million. This involved laying new floors throughout which gave a much lighter appearance. This was further improved by the provision of new ceilings with incorporated lighting.

Cladding and other new wall finishes were added, together with new signs and graphics to reflect the Centre's modern image. Improvements were made to most of the entrances and the area known as Cleveland Square was completely revamped, drawing all eyes to the main focal point, a one fifth-scale model of Captain Cook's ship, The Endeavour. Wall graphics depicting a seascape and harbour scene, and an attractive new feature, a map of one of Cook's voyages, was set in the floor and lit by fibre optics.

The continued commitment to investment has seen the centre develop as a major shopping destination for the wider Tees Valley, ensuring that The Mall, Middlesbrough, is a destination of choice for shopping as it should be.

Today, just as the area's premier shopping centre identifies itself closely with Cleveland's most famous son, it is not unreasonable to suppose that a 21st Century Captain Cook would be proud to identify himself with The Mall!

Left: *The model replica of Captain Cook's ship, The Endeavour.* ***Above:*** *Development of The Mall.* ***Below:*** *Interior views of The Mall, 2007.*

Atha And Co Solicitors - Experts On Our Doorstep

For most of us the law is a mystery. Yet sooner or later almost everyone is faced with a legal problem of some kind. Fortuntely help is at hand. The Middlesbrough firm of Atha and Co solicitors is well known to anyone who watches regional television, listens to local radio or travels on the buses in and around Middlesbrough.

Only in recent years however, has the legal profession been allowed to advertise its services to the public, and Atha and Co has been at the forefront of making its name known throughout the area.

Now a well-established brand leader in personal injury law the early days of laying the foundations. For that achievement were characterised not only by long hours and hard work but also by having access to all the necessary resources locally in Middlesbrough.

Local radio provided an excellent base for the new freedom to advertise. Radio's extensive local knowledge and technical expertise supported a campaign that soon made Atha and Co into a household name on Teesside.

The launch of Atha and Co onto the region's television screens was also made possible by a local TV production company, which meant that both creative and technical support services were available close at hand. As technology has continued to advance the company has continues to invest in its web facilities, not only providing a quick and easy way to get in touch 24 hours a day, but also including 'podcasts' which give users simple guides to understanding the process involved in making compensation claims.

Despite the march of new technology, continuity is evident at the Victorian premises of the firm's Middlesbrough office at 165 Albert Road which have been at the heart of Atha and Co for two decades. The central location between the University and the Law Courts has proved to be as convenient for 21st century clients as for their predecessors, with the city centre well served both by public transport and car parking. The addition of the MIMA building only adds to the prestige of the city to which Atha and Co is committed.

The story of Atha and Co began back in the early 1960s when Charles Atha's father Tony set up a Redcar branch of the

Top: *Tony Atha, founder of the business.* ***Left:*** *Atha & Co.'s 165 Albert Road, Middlesbrough, premises.* ***Right:*** *The reception area at Atha & Co.*

York-based solicitors Sykes, Johnson and Lee for whom he had originally worked as an articled clerk.

The Middlesbrough office would eventually employ five qualified solicitors, four experienced fee earners and a support staff of 30

Over a period of three years in a small first floor office suite in Redcar, and with the assistance of one secretary, Tony Atha conveyed over 300 properties on the Ings Farm Estate; and during that period also acquired a good number of private clients. When the estate was completed, as per a previous arrangement with Tony's partners, they vacated the partnership and left him as sole principal in the practice, which was now renamed Atha and Co.

Qualifying in 1958, after serving a two year stint of National Service, as an officer in the Army, Tony Atha was admitted as a solicitor of the Supreme Court of Judicature in 1960.

As a partner in what became Sykes, Lee and Atha Tony Atha quickly built up a network of offices across the area dealing primarily with the conveyancing of properties for local builders. With construction booming across Teesside throughout the 1960s and 70s the demand for conveyancing for both domestic and commercial properties was consistently high. Inevitably however, the recession that affected all of Britain in the years that followed also affected Teesside and led to a slowdown which persisted for some time. Happily the later trend of buy-to-let and later the introduction of the Government's Home Information Packs, would add to a steady flow of work, keeping Tony Atha and his team of conveyancing staff very busy serving both homeowners and investors.

Teesside's renowned chemical and manufacturing industries were also to feature in the development of

and to provide for their families. That local need was the impetus for a new focus within Atha and Co as the firm geared up to win compensation for thousands of accident and industrial disease victims amid an ever increasing awareness of health and safety issues.

The industrial disease and personal injury side of the practice built up steadily. Over a period of ten years or so the firm settled in excess of 15,000 industrial deafness and other related injuries for the people of Teesside recovering some £30 million in compensation. Eventually however the industrial disease work began to decline and the firm began to concentrate solely on personal injury claims. The firm successfully marketed a 'no win no fee' scheme and was years ahead of local competition in Middlesbrough. The firm likes to think that it constantly keeps at least two steps ahead of competitors whilst offering clients the best possible funding arrangements.

Atha and Co, when Tony's son Charles joined the practice in 1987 and began to take the firm in a new direction.

After Charles had taken his degree in law he had decided to serve his articles with the Newcastle firm of Ward Hadway. Whilst at that time Tony Atha was disappointed that his son chose to serve his articles with another firm, that choice would prove to be exactly the right decision, since it gave Charles an insight into fields of legal work not practised by his father's firm.

The legacy of industrial diseases left by decades of heavy manufacturing on Teesside left many victims suffering often painful and life-threatening conditions. They were entitled to compensation to help with costs of healthcare

Atha & Co became one of the first firms of solicitors in England to become a corporate body recognised by the Law Society

With Charles Atha at the helm the practice expanded rapidly to service that new work. The growing Middlesbrough office would eventually employ five qualified solicitors, four experienced fee earners and a supporting staff of 30.

Moving ever forward Atha & Co became one of the first firms of solicitors in England to become a corporate body recognised by the Law Society.

The 1990s saw tremendous changes to local industry as service sector jobs increased to replace the declining number of those in the

manufacturing sector: the firm continued to offer Personal Injury services to those seeking to claim compensation from any quarter.

Having established a knowledge base in Personal Injury Atha and Co has developed a team of specialists focussing exclusively in that area of law: working alongside Charles Atha, both as solicitors and company directors, are Rachel Maughan, Martin Demoily and Anna Guest. All the directors take an active role in the management of the business as well as having their own caseload. Regular team discussions allow the sharing of experience and joint problem solving, especially in new or particularly complex areas of law in a field which changes all the time. This level of personal involvement helps keep to a minimum the bureaucracy and red tape so often associated with the legal profession, and encourages a flexible and informal approach within the business.

Many clients are pleasantly surprised to have access to their own solicitor so easily, when modern business life has moved so far towards call centres and automated answering systems with several stages to get through before being able to speak to a real person. At Atha and Co direct personal contact is as much at the heart of business philosophy now as it has been since the firm began in the 1960s. Clients seem to agree: the overwhelming majority come through personal recommendation. This direct approach enables the firm to avoid the use of claims management companies or 'claims farmers' whose often-dubious methods and sometimes excessively large charges have been of such concern to both public and professionals alike. Experience from Atha's own clients indicates that people prefer to choose a solicitor for themselves based on reputation and experience rather than have one thrust upon them by a claims management company or an insurer.

Looking to the future the latest trend appears to be the advent of the Supermarket Solicitor dispensing legal advice alongside the weekly grocery shopping. Only time will tell whether this is what the public really wants, or whether, like the 'claims farmers', it will be consigned to history as yet another passing phase. As far as Atha and Co is concerned however, it remains committed to being accessible and available to all those people who need help. Whatever trends may come and go the firm's future will remain in Middlesbrough.

Pictures, both pages: *The Atha & Co. team: Anna Guest (top left), Martin Demoily (bottom left) Rachel Maughan (above) and Charles Atha (below).*

Parson & Crosland - Not Steel Alone

Based at Newport Works in Forty Foot Road, P&C Holdings Ltd, made up of Parson & Crosland Ltd and William Lane Ltd, is a Middlesbrough group whose scope down the years has stretched from the immediate locality to as far away as South America.

Parson & Crosland was started in 1926 by Hugh Crosland, and twin brothers Claude and Clyde Parson.

The three went into business to sell iron and steel materials and soon had offices, in London, Birmingham, Manchester, Glasgow, Swansea, Brussels and, not least, Middlesbrough. They also diversified their activities, buying out companies and offering management consultancy and long term loans to finance business.

During the world wide slump in the early 1930s offices had to close, directors' fees were cut and the two Parson brothers resigned, leaving Hugh Crosland as sole Managing Director. At this time, the Head Office was in River Plate House in the City of London and H Henderson was the Chairman.

The group's first dealings in South America were through Kenneth Henderson who opened the first office in Buenos Aires in 1926. This foothold in a foreign market proved an advantageous move as in those days it was difficult for foreign companies to get credit from European suppliers and Parson & Crosland acted as a confirming house.

In 1935 Evans Thornton became a limited company and Parson & Crosland took a 40 per cent of the shares in return for its existing Argentinean businesses, namely Philco and Lindley engineering. Philco Argentina would become one of the largest manufacturers of televisions and video recorders in the country.

After the end of the second world war there was a shortage of steel. In 1948 the company moved out of River Plate House. Things were difficult on the home market but Evans Thornton had a bumper year in 1947 due to the sale of 100 Gloster Meteor Jet Fighter aircraft for £4 million, the first aircraft of the Argentine airforce.

Evans Thornton was wound up as a holding company in 1978. The firm now owned a non-ferrous foundry Sacima (sold in 1996), the aircraft sales company Avietsa as well as some agencies which ceased trading after the Falklands Conflict of 1982. Avietsa is now involved in the automation business and sells robots and quick release couplings.

***Top left:** Hugh Crosland. **Left:** A Parson & Crosland custom built vehicle for travel to remote locations by railway track. **Above:** Lionel Butler Henderson and colleagues at work in South America.*

Back in the UK, the Middlesbrough office was run by Charles (later Sir Charles) Fitton, who had been made a director of the company in 1933. Almost the whole of the business was involved in the stocking of steel and iron. In those days this was not very sophisticated - in many cases a stockist simply had steel leaning against the walls of his warehouse, the ends of bars sunk into a channel in the ground. Bars were simply pulled away when required. Today stocks stand at around 6,000 tonnes, most of which are heavy structural steels.

In 1948, Hugh's son, Charles Crosland joined the company and was almost immediately sent to work in Argentina.

The 1950s was a time of expansion due to acquisitions. In 1951 Teesbank Ltd was bought in Middlesbrough, specialists in the testing and repairing of wrought iron, steel chains, wire rope slings and general lifting gear. That year also marked the 25th anniversary of the founding of the company, and one week's extra pay was awarded to the whole company.

Towards the end of the 1950s Charles Crosland and some Peruvian contacts formed Peru Mercantil, a trading company which started selling Rolls Royce Diesel engines. Later this company was to become Crosland Tecnica.

In 1966 the company bought its present site, the Newport Works, from Richard Hill and sold its lifting gear business. The following year Sir Charles Fitton died. In 1968 Ian Crane was made General Manager, becoming a director in 1977. At this time the non-ferrous foundry of William Lane was bought, having been established by the Lane family in the mid-Victorian era.

William Lane Ltd was founded by three Lanes, all of whom lived in Smith Street, Stockton: William Lane was a brass finisher, John Lane a brass moulder, and James Lane a blacksmith. Their original foundry was located in Middle Street Stockton and was set up in 1862.

In 1907 the business relocated to Forty Foot Road in Middlesbrough. The original buildings were timber framed with

Top left: *Coke furnace with lids, 1970s.* ***Above left:*** *A sand mould for an Impeller.* ***Below:*** *Sales office in 1966.* ***Bottom:*** *Parson & Crosland's premises, Forty Foot Road, early 1980s.*

three coke-fired furnaces built into the floor. In those days there were no cranes and everything was lifted by hand. The new site was in the heart of Middlesbrough's iron and steel making district. Many of the nearby businesses were customers for what was described as a 'breakdown and jobbing foundry'. Local steel-maker Corus remains an important customer.

A new foundry was constructed on the site in 1939. The original foundry is now used as a store for patterns. The new brick building had seven coke furnaces in the floor: these were still occasionally used until 2001.

The company remained in the hands of the Lane family until 1976, when it was sold to Parson & Crosland, although the founders' descendant Roy Lane stayed with the company until 1984. John Webb was appointed General Manager when it was taken over, and that year took on Stuart Duffy as a 15-year-old apprentice. Today Stuart is a director of the company.

Whilst many volume foundries have struggled to cope with competition from emerging economies such as China and gone out of business William Lane Ltd has stuck to its core competencies, providing bespoke castings on a short lead-time basis in any quantity from one upwards.

The furnaces have a capacity of up to 300kg, in a variety of metals: - Brasses, Bronzes, Aluminium, Gunmetal, Iron, and Copper. Customers range from architectural blacksmiths for intricate ironwork and renovation applications to pump manufacturers requiring impellers.

Fundamentally nothing has changed: the foundry products remain handmade by highly skilled tradesmen who work closely with clients to solve their engineering problems. Despite a traditional work ethic and output however investment in the future ensures modernity where it counts: two new electric induction furnaces have been installed as well as new cranes, shot blasting and sand mixing equipment, all of which have significantly improved efficiency.

Above: *A view of the steel stock holding warehouse in the 1960s.* ***Below left:*** *A Parson & Crosland exhibition in 1968.* ***Below:*** *Part of Parson & Crosland's transport fleet, 1966.*

By 1974, the year the office moved to Kingsway, London. Portman Hill moved to Middlesbrough and Parson & Crosland (Middlesbrough) Limited was formed.

Charles Crosland was killed in a tragic riding accident in 1995 and Ian Crane became Chairman and Managing Director of the Group. One year later and an offer was received from the firm's partners in Peru and Parson& Crosland shares in Crosland Tecnica were disposed of. The company continued its phase of consolidation into its core Middlesbrough-based activities. HE Wooley, the group's fire extinguisher and fire protection business, was sold to its manager Harry Wilmott in 2000 and moved off site two years later. Harry Wilmott also acquired P&C's participation in the South American business of Avietsa in this period. In the same year the stockholding business appointed a new Managing Director Edward Bilcliffe, previously a director for a national stockholding business.

During 2002 the Crosland family decided that they wanted to exit the remainder of the business; as a consequence during that year the Directors completed a management buy out of the company. P&C Holdings Ltd was formed for this purpose, holding the shares of the two Middlesbrough trading companies, of Parson & Crosland Ltd and of William Lane Ltd. The remaining export business, Portman Hill & Co Ltd, was sold off in the first half of 2003.

The company maintains a comprehensive range of steel products in stock, totalling in excess of 6,000 tonnes. With a 40,000 sq ft warehouse, an additional 35,000 sq ft of open gantry and extensive open free standing storage space, the firm also has the capacity to 'manage' projects, stored in bulk and delivered just in time.

Since the management buyout a substantial investment programme has been implemented. The property has been refurbished. A new steel plate profiling bay has been added, with refurbished gas machines, two new high definition plasma-cutting machines, and two new CNC plate drills. The company is now well equipped to provide a range of structural fittings to the buoyant construction sector, and components to engineering businesses. At the same time processing machinery has been installed to enhance the service offered for other products, most notably a CNC sawing and drilling line for structural sections.

The company now employs 50 staff in Middlesbrough, and is fully prepared, for the challenges ahead.

Top left: *The William Lane foundry, early 1990s.* ***Top right:*** *A replica Middlesbrough locomotive name plaque manufactured by the company which now hangs in the players tunnel at the Riverside Stadium.* ***Below:*** *Stuart Duffy (left), Steve Marlbrough (second right) and Dave Stewart (right) present the plaque for the players tunnel to the then Middlesbrough Manager Brian Robson.*

R C Ayres - Built to Last

In 1915, having completed his apprenticeship as a slater and tiler, Charles Henry Ayres purchased a handcart for three shillings and nine pence and so began the family business that still exists today. He set up his slating and tiling company in a small part of a large commercial site in Douglas Street, walking to his first jobs, pushing the handcart loaded with roofing materials. Luckily, he was a strong man, keen on bodybuilding and winner of third prize in a 'Mr. Yorkshire' bodybuilding contest.

By the 1920s Charlie Ayres was employing eight men. His eldest son, Ronald Cranston Ayres, followed in his father's footsteps, joining the business as an apprentice slater and tiler in the 1930s. When the Second World War broke out, Ron left the company to join the armed forces, along with his two younger brothers, Stanley Charles and Edgar. Charlie continued to work in the business until 1940 when, while his sons were away, he suffered a heart attack and died. The company ceased trading, but in 1946 Ron, who survived Dunkirk, was de-mobbed from the army. He decided to re-start the business under his own name, R.C. Ayres. He was joined for a short time by his brothers - Stan as a bricklayer, and Edgar as a wagon driver. Ron's wife, Nora, managed the office.

In the post-war years, Ron built a thriving business which saw a welcome development in the transportation of men and materials. In the days of the handcart, when jobs were carried out in Thornaby, a fortifying tea-break was taken before tackling the challenge of Brewery Bank.

Above left: *Founder Charles Henry Ayres.* ***Below:*** *Documentation of Charles Ayres' indentures for J&R Mascall Ltd, 1901.* ***Top right, facing page:*** *A keen sportsman Charles Ayres is pictured front right in the slaters and tilers football team pre 1914.* ***Centre right:*** *Pre-war plaques still on show at the company today.* ***Right:*** *Charles Ayres (in white sleeves) and a colleague on a roofing job in Bishop Auckland in 1910.*

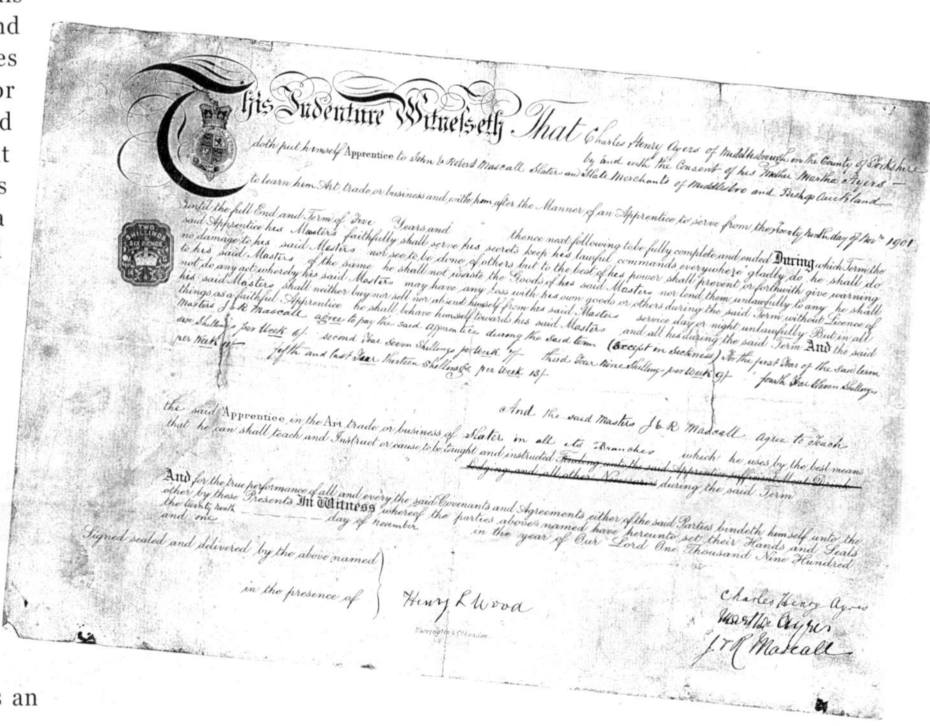

This Indenture Witnesseth That Charles Henry Ayers of Middlesbrough in the County of Yorkshire by and with the Consent of his Mother Martha Ayers doth put himself Apprentice to John & Robert Mascall Slater and Slate Merchants of Middlesbro and Bishop Auckland to learn him Art, trade or business and with him after the Manner of an Apprentice to serve from the twenty ninth day of Novr 1901 until the full End and Term of Five Years and thence next following to be fully complete and ended During which Term the said Apprentice his Masters faithfully shall serve his secrets keep his lawful commands everywhere gladly do he shall do no damage to his said Masters nor see to be done of others but to the best of his power shall prevent or forthwith give warning to his said Masters of the same he shall not waste the Goods of his said Masters nor lend them unlawfully to any he shall not do any act whereby his said Masters may have any loss with his own goods or others during the said Term without Licence of his said Masters shall neither buy nor sell nor absent himself from his said Masters service day or night unlawfully But in all things as a faithful Apprentice he shall behave himself towards his said Masters and all his during the said Term And the said Masters J & R Mascall agree to pay the said Apprentice during the said term (Except in sickness) For the first Year of the said term six Shillings per Week 6/- second Year Seven Shillings per Week 7/- third Year Nine Shillings per Week 9/- fourth Year Eleven Shillings per Week 11/- fifth and last Year Thirteen Shillings per Week 13/-

And the said Masters J & R Mascall agree to teach the said Apprentice in the Art trade or business of Slater in all its Branches which he uses by the best means that he can shall teach and Instruct or cause to be taught and instructed ~~Finding unto the said Apprentice sufficient Meat Drink Lodging and all other Necessaries~~ during the said Term

And for the true performance of all and every the said Covenants and Agreements either of the said Parties bindeth himself unto the other by these Presents In Witness whereof the parties above named have hereunto set their Hands and Seals the twenty ninth day of November in the year of Our Lord One Thousand Nine Hundred and one

Signed sealed and delivered by the above named in the presence of Henry L Wood

Charles Henry Ayres
Martha Ayres
J & R Mascall

The Company carried out major building and roofing works for a variety of clients including heavy industry, commercial enterprises and Local Authority domestic and heritage projects. Head Wrightson's Steel Foundry and Scottish and Newcastle Breweries were two of the important clients who used R.C. Ayres' services for many years. In 1962, as part of their work refurbishing the Coatham Hotel in Redcar, the company removed the gun turrets erected during the First World War from the hotel tower.

Attracting a growing and loyal workforce, the company acquired a reputation for specialist roofing skills and excellent workmanship. Ted Dunn and Joe McMahon underwent their apprenticeship as slaters and tilers at R.C. Ayres and went on to spend their whole working lives with the company, notching up over 90 years between them. They took Ronald's son, Alan Charles, under their wing when he became, in 1962, the third generation to work in the family firm. Alan, the current owner and managing director of the company, remembers how different life in the building and roofing industry was when he started work. There was a lime pit in the yard where lime was slaked ready for use and bricks arrived still hot from Coatham Stob Brickworks and all had to be unloaded and stacked by hand. Mechanical and motorised assistance with lifting and moving heavy gear wasn't as readily available as it is now. Work was hard but there was camaraderie among the men and lots of good humour.

C.H.AYRES.
SLATER ETC.

R.C. AYRES.
BUILDER & SLATER

1946 INCORPORATED
RC AYRES LTD 1961

When Ron became ill in 1972, Alan took over the running of the business. The company continued to grow and gradually acquired the whole Douglas Street site, land and buildings, including Brine Wells Garage which was accessible from Borough Road. Joinery goods were manufactured on site and motor mechanics employed to maintain vehicles, plant and equipment.

The skills of Ted, Joe, George Barrass (bricklayer), Bob Eden and Bill Earl (joiners), Tommy Wardle (general foreman) and many other long-serving employees, meant that the company won a number of prestigious orders. In 1984, it was presented with a Civic Award for the restoration of the original Middlesbrough Town Hall. A year later, the company completely re-roofed Middlesbrough's Central Library, an impressive architectural addition to the town, courtesy of the philanthropist, Andrew Carnegie. Constantine College, where Alan had studied building and management, was another edifice to benefit from the traditional building and roofing skills which were the trademark of the company.

In more recent times, the business was highly commended in the National Heritage Awards for the restoration of Ivy Cottage, a long house in Cowpen Bewley and the oldest dwelling house in Cleveland. This was a Cleveland Preservation Society project. The Analytical Chemists, Ridsdale and Co., also needed a company that had retained traditional slating skills when Newham Hall at Newby required work on the old Westmoreland slated roof. Alongside these skills, R.C.Ayres kept up with modern developments and was at the forefront of the flat roofing revolution.

Above: *Re-roofing and refurbishment of the County Hotel in Newport Road in the late 1950s.* ***Left:*** *Alan Ayres and Keith Lamb, Chief Executive, of MFC, (the football club has been a client since the early 1960s) in front of the Ayresome Park Gates which were re erected 2005. The brick columns supporting the gates have a number of bricks which were originally in the walls at the Holgate end of the old Ayresome Park Ground.*

More durable single ply P.V.C. membranes are now replacing the traditional felt roofing products. Alan and a number of employees went to Switzerland in 1983 for training in the use of such advanced products and have since used them regularly to cure leaky flat roofs on schools, hospitals and vast areas such as the 15,000 square metre roof of Next Distribution warehouses near Tilbury Docks.

The dual focus - building and roofing - of this family firm continues to this day. Another loyal employee, Paul Pugh, who has been with the company since 1980, now manages the building element, running major contracts within the chemical complexes at Wilton and Billingham. One such contract in 2006 was to provide the civils infrastructure for the state-of-the-art tomato growing glass houses at Billingham.

Family is a recurring theme in the business. The company has worked for well-known Middlesbrough families such as Newboulds, Uptons, Sparks and Hintons. As Alan's son, Michael, and daughter, Rachael, have worked at Douglas Street during their student days, four generations have now worked for the company. Ann and Sue, sisters of Alan's wife, Elizabeth, are part of the administrative support team in the company offices.

Alan feels that his involvement with the current Erimus Decent Homes Project has brought the company, in some respects, full circle, as some of the houses Ron Ayres tiled in Linthorpe are now being repaired and re-roofed by the company some seventy years later. They have, like the company stood the test of time.

Above: *Second generation Ron Ayres, far right and third generation Alan Ayres, second from right, present workers Joe McMahon and Ted Dunn with 25 years service watches, 1978.* ***Left:*** *Refurbishment of the Old Town Hall, Middlesbrough which gained the company a Civic Award in 1984.* ***Below:*** *Paul Pugh, Contracts Manager, checking the concrete plinths on the recently constructed pipe line for Terra Industries, supplying the tomato plant at Billingham with steam and electricity.*

Greco Brothers - Ice is Nice but Cornets Count

Middlesbrough gained fame for its iron and steel, but it was hot work. So what better than an ice-cream to quench the heat? And you can bet that the cornet was made locally by Greco Brothers Ltd.

Liberato Greco was born in Arpino, just south of Rome. The town was the birthplace of the famous Roman orator Cicero, but Liberato decided that the burgeoning ice cream industry, not oratory, was the career for him. Italy was the birthplace of the world's ice-cream industry. Thousands of Italians left their homeland taking the delights of ice-cream to every country on earth. In 1907 Liberato and his brothers, Antonio and Tullio came to Britain. Here he began to sell ices from a hand barrow. Soon he graduated to a horse and cart and later still to a motor bicycle and sidecar.

In the early 1920s Liberato decided to set up in business on his own in Suffield Street, Middlesbrough. After a year or two a change was made from making ice cream to manufacturing wafers and cornets. In all these enterprises, Liberato was helped by Antonio and Tullio. The work was hard, involving manual methods of manufacture and the hours were long. But their hard work paid off and provided a living for themselves and succeeding generations. Liberato's daughter, Hilda, learned her father's trade and demonstrated the same attitude of commitment as Liberato and his brothers had done.

Ironically and tragically Liberato would be deprived of his liberty during the second world war. The male members of the Greco family, as citizens of an enemy country, were interned. All the three brothers were aboard the Andorra Star as internees, on their way to Canada, when the ship was torpedoed by a German U-boat and sunk in mid-Atlantic. Five hundred miles out from Ireland, a destroyer, the St Lawrence, picked up survivors who had been in the sea for over six hours. Sadly one of the brothers, Tullio, was lost in the cold waters. The St Lawrence returned all survivors, including Liberato and Antonio, back to Britain.

Liberato's daughter, Hilda, had been capably running the business for him in his absence. Back from the sea Liberato was able to take over the reins of the business once more. A few years later Hilda married a fellow Italian, Laurence Antonio Rovardi, who would make his own valuable contribution to the firm. The

Top left: *Founder, Liberato Greco in his Ford van, Albert Park.* ***Above:*** *Liberato selling ices from his motor bicycle and side-car, 1926.* ***Below left:*** *making cornets the old way.* ***Below:*** *Tony Rovardi pictured in the early 1950s.*

couple's sons, Peter and Lawrence, continued the family tradition of running the business to the third generation. Lawrence, incidentally, was so-named after the ship which picked up his grandfather and great uncle during the war.

In 1980 the company was looking towards modernisation and expansion, so a move was made from its original premises in Suffield Street to the company's present modern factory location in Greta Street. Nowadays, using state of the art cone and wafer ovens, the firm manufactures products to sell to many wholesale ice cream manufacturers and retail outlets throughout the UK.

The product range is far more extensive than in the past. The customer is almost spoilt for choice confronted with the delights of thick and crispy chocolate wafers, nougat wafers, oyster shells, sugar cones, twin cones and single cones in a variety of sizes as well as many other products used by the ice cream trade.

As a result of increased demand the factory premises have been extended to include the land previously occupied by Middlesbrough School. Part of the Old School Complex, as it is known, is rented out to other local businesses as well as incorporating the enlarged cone production area and storage facility.

Many of us have enjoyed Greco Brothers' products without being aware of it. That the company with humble beginnings has survived and grown so much over the years is testimony to the commitment and dedication of the Greco brothers and the succeeding generations of the family.

Now Peter's son, Tony has taken on the role filled by Lawrence until his retirement in 2001.

Meanwhile Tony and Hilda (Lawrence and Peter's Rovardi's parents) have now returned to Arpino in Italy to live, and to explain to the descendants of Cicero exactly why it is that ice-cream cones and wafers made in Middlesbrough are the best in the world.

Top left: *Liberato with his grandson Lawrence.* ***Bottom left:*** *Batter mixing in 1952.* ***Top centre:*** *Peter and Lawrence exhibiting at an ice cream convention, 1990s.* ***Left:*** *A view inside the Greco Brothers warehouse, 2001.* ***Below:*** *Peter Rovardi and son Tony outside the company premises.*

Hertel UK Ltd - Providing Total Service Solutions

Hertel UK Ltd, whose head office is based at Sotherby Road, Skippers Lane Industrial Estate, Middlesbrough, has been an important part of the local scene since the 1970s. The company is, however, just one within the Hertel family of firms which form part of an international group of companies.

The Hertel business was founded in Amsterdam on 1st August 1895 by Alexander C.L. Hertel; he started a small enterprise specialising in the production of insulation material. Today that once small business has grown to become a major European wide enterprise.

Alexander Hertel, the son of German immigrants to the USA, was born on 17th July 1865, in Boston, Massachusetts. As a young man he became a sailor, plying the North Atlantic trade routes, before deciding that a land-based career was preferable to a life on the ocean waves.

Working as a one-man operator from 101 Prins Hendrikekade in Amsterdam, Hertel's original business activity was selling gaskets and insulation material to the shipping industry. The company very soon acquired a good name as a reliable and quality-conscious supplier for shipyards in Northern Europe. In 1912 Hertel's growing firm became a private limited company. It was perhaps not the best of times to form a new company as two years later the first world war broke out. Shipping and international trade was inevitably badly disrupted.

The1920s would see an upswing in trade only to be followed by the collapse of world trade in the 1930s and a much reduced demand for shipping. The second world war which broke out in 1939 posed additional problems. Holland was invaded, the British Navy blockaded European ports and raw materials which might have gone to commerce were directed towards the German war effort. Happily the firm survived these difficult times and was able to take full advantage of the postwar upswing.

During the 20th century the firm repeatedly stepped early into new markets to meet the needs of the customers, and into innovative technological developments. Consequently the company was able to keep going through times of crisis and various periods of economic decline.

Following the founder's death the company was managed by Alexander's son, Keype Hertel, who ran the firm until 1957. Family members remained on the company's supervisory board until 1972.

1975 saw the company expand its business into the United Kingdom and open its first office in Middlesbrough.

Today Hertel employs over 3,800 people in the UK and has offices throughout the country.

In the twenty first century Hertel has become a substantial, international enterprise. It has grown into a company that specialises in the construction, maintenance and dismantling of industrial installations in the oil & gas, chemical and power industry. For the defence & offshore market Hertel designs, supplies and installs technical specialised modular units. Internationally Hertel has a workforce of over 6,500 employees. It combines integrated services with operational expertise, flexibility and service. The company has a great deal of experience in preparation, coordination, implementation, new-build and maintenance works, with a wide-ranging array of services that includes insulation and trace heating, scaffolding construction, painting and spraying, asbestos removal and fire protection.

2007 saw Hertel not only operating from the UK, but also from the Netherlands, Belgium, Germany, Ireland, Poland France, Lithuania, Romania, China, Kuwait, Dubai, Singapore, Thailand and Canada. After over a century of providing services, the company has established a strong position in a variety of market sectors. These include petrochemicals, power stations, power supplies, pharmaceuticals and shipbuilding.

A major strength of Hertel is its policy of constant innovation. Its customers can also rely on operationally secure implementation and delivery.

Hertel is happy to relieve all their customers' concerns about maintenance, coordination and consultation.

The business is a remarkable legacy of that young American sailor who forsook the sea in the reign of Queen Victoria for a life of land bound commerce. Alexander Hertel could surely never have envisaged back in 1895 when he walked the streets of Amsterdam in search of customers that his one-man enterprise would grow to be an international group of companies with thousands of employees. Alexander Hertel was, however, surely someone who truly deserved that ultimate business accolade of being dubbed a genuine entrepreneur.

Top left: *Founder, Alexander C.L. Hertel.* ***Left:*** *An early 20th century view of the Hertel Amsterdam site.* ***Above:*** *Hertel UK Ltd's Skippers Lane Industrial Estate site, 2007.* ***Right:*** *On site providing total service solutions.*

St Mary's College
Over a Century of Academic Achievement

In 1904, in response to a rapid expansion in the Roman Catholic population in the Middlesbrough district, Bishop Lacy invited the Society of Mary (hitherto based in London) to found a school in a building previously used as a hospital at the junction of the Avenue and Eastbourne Road, in the village of Linthorpe. The first short-lived headmaster was Fr. Watters who felt the school was doomed to fail and he was superseded in 1906 by Fr. Moran.

The school grew very slowly. By 1910 St Mary's had only 67 pupils. Father Moran was undaunted and organised a full programme for the pupils he did have, complete with Prize-giving and Sports Day. The school was loyally supported by the clergy and parish. Most North Riding boys came on 'Bishop's Scholarships' and not many pupils paid full fees. Numbers began to grow. By 1918 a total of 100 boys was reached, some of them boarders, and by 1920 there were 160 day boys, 20 boarders and the school was only £500 in the red at the bank.

At the beginning of the First World War the school had to close until its cellars had been reinforced to make them into safe air-raid shelters. Because the school had Direct Grant status, no government grants were available for this.

In 1922 Father William Fox became headmaster. He knew the school well, having been an assistant master for 14 years. More and more pupils continued to arrive and the need for

Top left: *Fr. James Moran, S.M., the 'real founder' of St Mary's College, Middlesbrough.* ***Above:*** *The College in The Avenue.* ***Below:*** *The staff as seen in 1927.*

extra classrooms had been met by the acquisition of several army huts in 1919. They had good use made of them on Saturdays for extra classes in woodwork, art, shorthand and music.

In 1923 the school's catchment area was increased. The Bishop was quietly using it as a junior seminary, and successfully, judging by the number of old boys who entered the priesthood.

By the thirties most pupils were accommodated in a large house. Behind this was the school gymnasium. A row of huts which separated two paved areas were still being used. One tree on the area required for the paved yard was so venerable that instructions were given to pave around it. Beyond the buildings was the playing field.

Soon a single storey building was put up on the old playing field which provided specialist rooms for art, chemistry and physics. When a new church was built, the old one became a

general-purpose building. New playing fields were acquired out at Saltersgill, where pupils had to change in a draughty old cabin.

After the war, academic results improved and numbers increased. School dinners and school milk made their appearance. At this time, St Mary's lost its Direct Grant status and became 'voluntary assisted'. The local authority was generous in supplying equipment.

A new college building was begun on the playing fields at Saltersgill. Classes moved out there as rooms became available. Since the two buildings were more than a mile apart, putting together the timetable became a nightmare. The school roll increased again so, inevitably, there were more huts. Building began again on an adjacent site.

In the schools' reorganisation of the early 1970s, St Mary's became a co-educational sixth form college. The management hoped that the spirit of its past would prevail. At first the girls from the Convent and the boys from St Mary's were in two opposing camps, but in their self-imposed blue denim uniforms the two groups soon merged, worked together and endured together the 1975/76 modernisation when lorries and mobile cranes trundled past classroom windows.

Since then St. Mary's has increased in stature. It is now Middlesbrough's only sixth form college and has acquired a justified reputation for academic excellence whilst ensuring that students can benefit from a wide range of extra-curricular activities, trips and visits.

The Ofsted inspection report in 2007 highlighted as key strengths the College's 'living vibrant Catholic ethos', 'strong focus on improving the quality of teaching and learning', 'good individual support for students', and 'excellent progression to higher education'.

Above left: *Today's advanced equipment.* ***Above:*** *A view inside the LRC, 2007.* ***Below:*** *St Mary's College, 2007.*

Suggitt's - Real Ice-Cream

A Suggitt Ltd is a business name that few readers will instantly recognise: but mention Suggitt's Quality Ices and recognition is instant. The name Suggitt and ice-cream have been synonymous with one another for the better part of a century.

Suggitt's Quality Ices based at 93 High Street Great Ayton have been tickling taste buds since 1921.

Ice cream making started after Arthur Suggitt and his wife Bertha opened a confectionary shop at 14-15 High Green and Mrs Suggitt began making ice-cream at the weekends. It would be Bertha Suggitt who would subsequently be remembered as the founder of the future ice-cream enterprise.

In those far off days there were no domestic fridges or freezers. Blocks of ice were collected from the docks, crushed and added to brine to reduce their temperature still further. The salted ice could be used to freeze ice-cream and to cool storage freezers.

Though in later years dried milk powder could be obtained in the early days fresh milk had to be simmered overnight to evaporate some of the water, creating a thicker liquid for use in the ice-cram making process

Meanwhile Mrs Suggitt had more than ice-cream to worry about. Alan Suggitt who would eventually take the business to new heights of success was born in 1922.

Like all young boys Alan looked forward to a future with lots of ice cream in it. In 1939 however, the outbreak of the second world war would see ice–cream production halted due to the shortage of ice. It was not until 1945 that production began again.

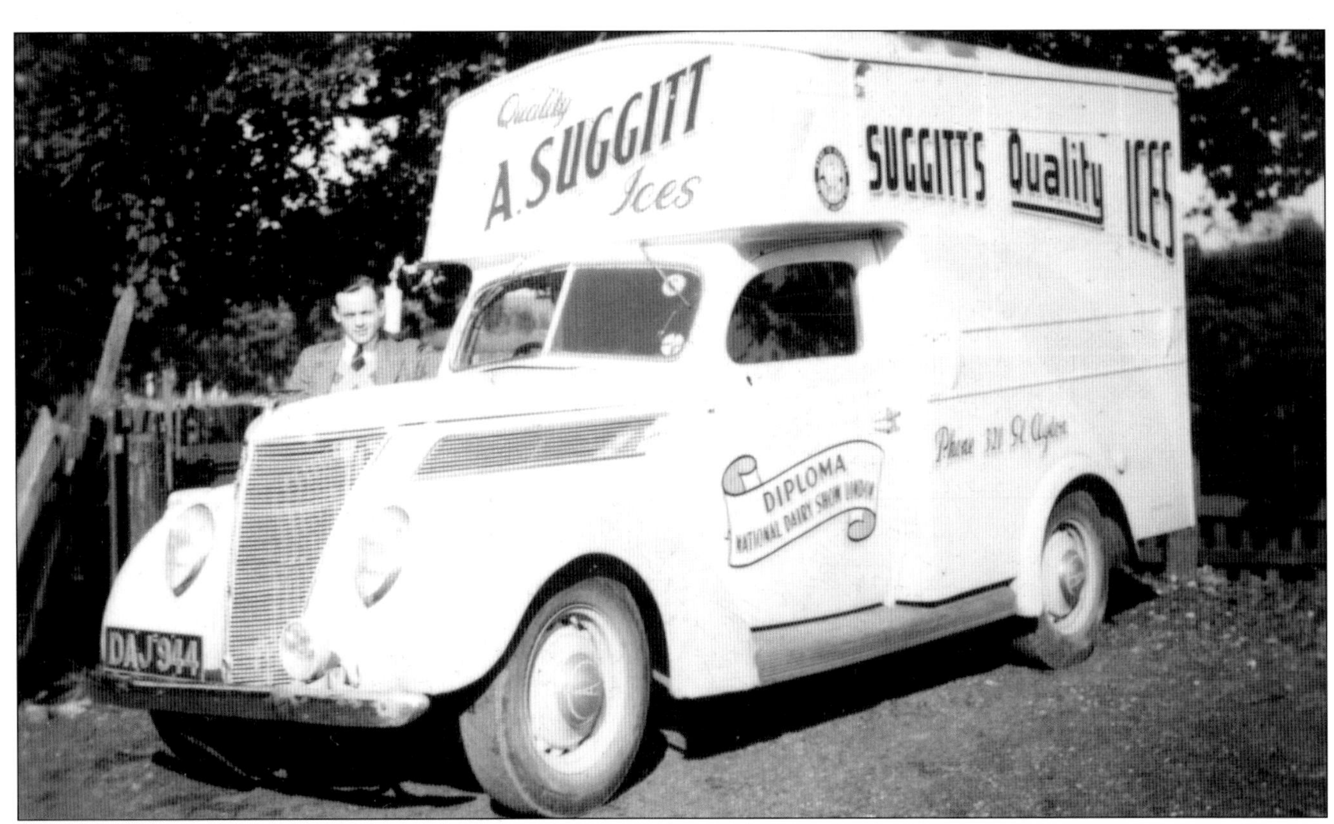

By the mid-1970s everyone who visited Great Ayton was dropping in at Suggitt's increasingly famous sweetshop and café for a cup of coffee or tea, or better still a wafer or cornet of Suggitt's distinctive ice-cream. According to Alan Suggitt who had seen the premises double in size "it's more like a club for local people than a café because it's quiet and pleasant. We don't have anything like juke boxes to shatter the peace."

Alan and Joyce's son Alan Peter Suggitt worked with his parents in the business until 1975 when he joined the Royal Air Force. As result the firm's second ice cream van was no longer used.

By 1956 ice cream production moved from behind the confectionary shop to new premises next to Greenbank.

Five years later the shop was extend into the former house next door and the original shop was turned over to storage.

When he was old enough Alan Suggitt would visit local beauty spots with his motorcycle and sidecar. The sidecar loaded with ice-cream for sale. The motorcycle would eventually give way to a van with weekend routs around Great Ayton and Stokesley giving way to a regular spot on the Plane at Stokesley and later at West Green. A second van was bought to go around local farms and villages as well as local village shows held in such places as Castleton, Danby and Killdale.

Bertha May Suggitt, a native of Stockton, who had moved to Great Ayton after leaving school, died in 1964. She would be remembered by thousands of people from a very wide area who had been served by her with ice-cram on their visits to the village. Following her death the limited company A Suggitt Ltd was formed

The business would now pass to Alan Suggitt and his wife Joyce who would run the café, ice-cream making operation and two ice-cream vans. Many folk will recall both Alan and Joyce dispensing ice-cream form their ice-cream vans in and around Stokesley for many years.

Change came in 1971 when fire damaged the old shop. It was demolished and a café added to the business.

Peter Suggitt who now runs the business returned from the RAF to join the family in 1987.

The last ice-cram van was disposed of in 1988 at the same time as Joyce Suggitt retired.

Alan Suggit died in 2001; sadly, Joyce followed him in 2002.

Today Peter Suggitt continues the fine family tradition begun by his grandmother Bertha Suggitt in the 1920s. Her winning recipe ensures that serious ice-cream aficionados still to flock to Great Ayton to experience ice-cream just like it used to taste.

SUGGITT'S...
Quality Ices
93 High Street
GREAT AYTON

Top left, facing page: *Mr Alan Suggitt.* ***Far left:*** *Alan Suggitt pictured alongside one of the company's ice-cream vans.* ***Top left:*** *Suggitt's ice -cream van at a local village show.* ***Above:*** *A familiar sight to the people of Middlesbrough, this image has been in use on Suggitt bags since the 1950s.*

ACKNOWLEDGMENTS

The publishers would like to sincerely thank the following for their help and contribution to this publication:

The staff at Middlesbrough Central Library

The staff at Redcar Central Library

The Northern Echo

Beamish Museum

The Imperial War Museum

Corus

Dr Barry Doyle - Corus story

Teesside Archives - Corus Photographs

The Dorman Museum

David Hunter and the 500 Group

Norman Moorsom

Paul Stephenson

Mrs Brion

Mr Warne

Colin Greenwell

Andrew Mitchell

Steve Ainsworth

Seamus Molloy

True North Books Ltd - Book List

Memories of Accrington - 1 903204 05 4
Memories of Barnet - 1 903204 16 X
Memories of Barnsley - 1 900463 11 3
More Memories of Barnsley - 1 903 204 79 8
Golden Years of Barnsley -1 900463 87 3
Memories of Basingstoke - 1 903204 26 7
Memories of Bedford - 1 900463 83 0
More Memories of Bedford - 1 903204 33 X
Golden Years of Birmingham - 1 900463 04 0
Birmingham Memories - 1 903204 45 3
More Birmingham Memories - 1 903204 80 1
Memories of Blackburn - 1 900463 40 7
More Memories of Blackburn - 1 900463 96 2
Memories of Blackpool - 1 900463 21 0
Memories of Bolton - 1 900463 45 8
More Memories of Bolton - 1 900463 13 X
Bolton Memories - 1 903204 37 2
Memories of Bournemouth -1 900463 44 X
Memories of Bradford - 1 900463 00 8
More Memories of Bradford - 1 900463 16 4
More Memories of Bradford II - 1 900463 63 6
Bradford Memories - 1 903204 47 X
More Bradford Memories - 1 903204 92 5
Bradford City Memories - 1 900463 57 1
Memories of Bristol - 1 900463 78 4
More Memories of Bristol - 1 903204 43 7
Memories of Bromley - 1 903204 21 6
Memories of Burnley - 1 900463 95 4
Golden Years of Burnley - 1 900463 67 9
Memories of Bury - 1 900463 90 3
More Memories of Bury - 1 903 204 78 X
Memories of Cambridge - 1 900463 88 1
Memories of Cardiff - 1 900463 14 8
More Memories of Cardiff - 1 903204 73 9
Memories of Carlisle - 1 900463 38 5
Memories of Chelmsford - 1 903204 29 1
Memories of Cheltenham - 1 903204 17 8
Memories of Chester - 1 900463 46 6
More Memories of Chester -1 903204 02 X
Chester Memories - 1 903204 83 6
Memories of Chesterfield -1 900463 61 X
More Memories of Chesterfield - 1 903204 28 3

Memories of Colchester - 1 900463 74 1
Nostalgic Coventry - 1 900463 58 X
Coventry Memories - 1 903204 38 0
Memories of Croydon - 1 900463 19 9
More Memories of Croydon - 1 903204 35 6
Golden Years of Darlington - 1 900463 72 5
Nostalgic Darlington - 1 900463 31 8
Darlington Memories - 1 903204 46 1
Memories of Derby - 1 900463 37 7
More Memories of Derby - 1 903204 20 8
Memories of Dewsbury & Batley - 1 900463 80 6
Memories of Doncaster - 1 900463 36 9
More Memories of Doncaster - 1 903204 75 5
Nostalgic Dudley - 1 900463 03 2
Golden Years of Dudley - 1 903204 60 7
Memories of Edinburgh - 1 900463 33 4
More memories of Edinburgh - 1903204 72 0
Memories of Enfield - 1 903204 14 3
Memories of Exeter - 1 900463 94 6
Memories of Glasgow - 1 900463 68 7
More Memories of Glasgow - 1 903204 44 5
Memories of Gloucester - 1 903204 04 6
Memories of Grimsby - 1 900463 97 0
More Memories of Grimsby - 1 903204 36 4
Memories of Guildford - 1 903204 22 4
Memories of Halifax - 1 900463 05 9
More Memories of Halifax - 1 900463 06 7
Golden Years of Halifax - 1 900463 62 8
Nostalgic Halifax - 1 903204 30 5
Memories of Harrogate - 1 903204 01 1
Memories of Hartlepool - 1 900463 42 3
Memories of High Wycombe - 1 900463 84 9
Memories of Huddersfield - 1 900463 15 6
More Memories of Huddersfield - 1 900463 26 1
Golden Years of Huddersfield - 1 900463 77 6
Nostalgic Huddersfield - 1 903204 19 4
Huddersfield Memories - 1903204 86 0
Huddersfield Town FC - 1 900463 51 2
Memories of Hull - 1 900463 86 5
More Memories of Hull - 1 903204 06 2
Hull Memories - 1 903204 70 4
Memories of Keighley - 1 900463 01 6

True North Books Ltd - Book List

Golden Years of Keighley - 1 900463 92 X
Memories of Kingston - 1 903204 24 0
Memories of Leeds - 1 900463 75 X
More Memories of Leeds - 1 900463 12 1
Golden Years of Leeds - 1 903204 07 0
Leeds Memories - 1 903204 62 3
More Leeds Memories - 1 903204 90 9
Memories of Leicester - 1 900463 08 3
More Memories of Leicester - 1 903204 08 9
Memories of Leigh - 1 903204 27 5
Memories of Lincoln - 1 900463 43 1
Memories of Liverpool - 1 900463 07 5
More Memories of Liverpool - 1 903204 09 7
Liverpool Memories - 1 903204 53 4
More Liverpool Memories - 1 903204 88 7
Memories of Luton - 1 900463 93 8
Memories of Macclesfield - 1 900463 28 8
Memories of Manchester - 1 900463 27 X
More Memories of Manchester - 1 903204 03 8
Manchester Memories - 1 903204 54 2
More Manchester Memories - 1 903204 89 5
Memories of Middlesbrough - 1 900463 56 3
More Memories of Middlesbrough - 1 903204 42 9
Middlesbrough & Teesside Memories - 1 903204 97 6
Memories of Newbury - 1 900463 79 2
Memories of Newcastle - 1 900463 81 4
More Memories of Newcastle - 1 903204 10 0
Newcastle Memories - 1.903204 71 2
Memories of Newport - 1 900463 59 8
Memories of Northampton - 1 900463 48 2
More Memories of Northampton - 1 903204 34 8
Memories of Norwich - 1 900463 73 3 .
Memories of Nottingham - 1 900463 91 1
More Memories of Nottingham - 1 903204 11 9
Nottingham Memories - 1 903204 63 1
Bygone Oldham - 1 900463 25 3
Memories of Oldham - 1 900463 76 8
More Memories of Oldham - 1 903204 84 4
Memories of Oxford - 1 900463 54 7
Memories of Peterborough - 1 900463 98 9
Golden Years of Poole - 1 900463 69 5
Memories of Portsmouth - 1 900463 39 3
More Memories of Portsmouth - 1 903204 51 8
Nostalgic Preston - 1 900463 50 4
More Memories of Preston - 1 900463 17 2
Preston Memories - 1 903204 41 0
Memories of Reading - 1 900463 49 0
Memories of Rochdale - 1 900463 60 1
More Memories of Reading - 1 903204 39 9
More Memories of Rochdale - 1 900463 22 9
Memories of Romford - 1 903204 40 2
Memories of Rothertham- 1903204 77 1
Memories of St Albans - 1 903204 23 2
Memories of St Helens - 1 900463 52 0
Memories of Sheffield - 1 900463 20 2
More Memories of Sheffield - 1 900463 32 6
Golden Years of Sheffield - 1 903204 13 5
Sheffield Memories - 1 903204 61 5
More Sheffield Memories - 1 903204 91 7
Memories of Slough - 1 900 463 29 6
Golden Years of Solihull - 1 903204 55 0
Memories of Southampton - 1 900463 34 2
More Memories of Southampton - 1 903204 49 6
Memories of Stockport - 1 900463 55 5
More Memories of Stockport - 1 903204 18 6
Stockport Memories - 1 903204 87 9
Memories of Stockton - 1 900463 41 5
Memories of Stoke-on-Trent - 1 900463 47 4
More Memories of Stoke-on-Trent - 1 903204 12 7
Memories of Stourbridge - 1903204 31 3
Memories of Sunderland - 1 900463 71 7
More Memories of Sunderland - 1 903204 48 8
Sunderland Memories - 1 903 204 95 X
Memories of Swindon - 1 903204 00 3
Memories of Uxbridge - 1 900463 64 4
Memories of Wakefield - 1 900463 65 2
More Memories of Wakefield - 1 900463 89 X
Nostalgic Walsall - 1 900463 18 0
Golden Years of Walsall - 1 903204 56 9
More Memories of Warrington - 1 900463 02 4
Warrington Memories - 1 903204 85 2
Memories of Watford - 1 900463 24 5
Golden Years of West Bromwich - 1 900463 99 7
Memories of Wigan - 1 900463 85 7
Golden Years of Wigan - 1 900463 82 2
More Memories of Wigan - 1 903204 82 8
Nostalgic Wirral - 1 903204 15 1
Wirral Memories - 1 903204 747
Memories of Woking - 1 903204 32 1
Nostalgic Wolverhampton - 1 900463 53 9
Wolverhampton Memories - 1 903204 50 X
Memories of Worcester - 1 903204 25 9
Memories of Wrexham - 1 900463 23 7
Memories of York - 1 900463 66 0
More Memories of York - 1 903 204 94 1

Available in the Local Interest section of all major bookshops or direct from the publishers - telephone 01422 344344